Pastor Don Matzat has the right response for those who find themselves wallowing in the ever-rising flood of books on humanistic psychology. Their question, generally, is "Who Are We and Why Are We So Unhappy?"

Mankind does not *have* a problem, mankind *is* the problem Only Jesus Christ can be the solution.

By making a sharp distinction between Christianity and good psychotherapy, *CHRIST-ESTEEM* helps to clear up the confusion which exists in the minds of many today.

The truly positive self-image, Matzat argues correctly, comes from knowing our sinful nature so that we will turn from ourselves to Jesus.

—D. James Kennedy, Ph.D.
Senior Minister
Coral Ridge Presbyterian Church
Fort Lauderdale, Florida

CHRIST ESTEEM

Don Matzat

HARVEST HOUSE PUBLISHERS
Eugene, Oregon 97402

CHRIST-ESTEEM

Library of Congress Cataloging-in-Publication Data

Matzat, Don.
    Christ-Esteem / Don Matzat.
    ISBN 0-89081-784-7
      1. Identification (Religion)   I. Title.
BV4509.5.M335   1990
248.4--dc20   89-27039
                                                  CIP

Printed in the United States of America.

TO MY FATHER
Whose faith, sacrifice, and commitment
made it possible for me
to enter the pastoral ministry.
"Cast your bread upon
the water...."

Contents

Introduction

1. A Challenging Generation 15

2. An Irrelevant Gospel? 25

3. Knowing Yourself 37

4. The Right Diagnosis 47

5. Identified with Adam 59

6. Turning Away from Self 71

7. Identified with Christ 87

8. Everything in Christ 101

9. The Conflict 117

10. Looking unto Jesus 129

11. Confessing Truth 143

12. Rejoice in the Lord! 153

13. Jesus Is the Life! 167

14. Christians Under Construction 179

15. The Identity of the Christian Community .. 195

Notes

Introduction

"Any fusion of the respective goals
of religion and psychotherapy
must result in confusion."
—Dr. Viktor Frankl

In 1956, Dr. William Hulme began his book *Counseling and Theology* by saying:

> Pastoral counseling in its present form is a new development within the church. Pastors who have celebrated their twenty-fifth anniversary of their ordination heard little if anything about it in their seminary days.... In former days the pastor's counseling was oriented in pastoral theology; today it centers in pastoral psychology.[1]

On the first page of their 1979 book titled *The Integration of Psychology and Theology,* Bruce Narramore and John D. Carter write:

> Christianity is in the throes of an encounter with psychology. On academic and popular levels alike, psychology is making inroads into areas traditionally considered the domain of Christianity. And the signs of this encounter are everywhere about us. Religious bookstores are filled with volumes on psychology....[2]

A major controversy exists in the Christian church today over the issue of mixing the principles of secular psychology with the truths of Christian theology. A great deal has been written over the past ten years either condemning or encouraging the integration of the two disciplines. While each Christian denomination might have its own particular conflicts, all of them have to one degree or another debated this subject.

The intrusion of secular psychology into Christian teaching and counseling indicates a lack within the proclamation of the Christian church. A void obviously exists which is being filled by the offerings of psychology. The question is, a lack of what? Where does the void exist? There are two possibilities.

On the one hand, there may be a lack in the content of biblical Christianity itself which requires the addition of psychology. If this is the case, psychology should be welcomed into the church in order to help us meet the needs of hurting people. It may actually be a wonderful gift of our heavenly Father given to us out of love for his psychologically bruised and emotionally damaged children.

But on the other hand, there may be a lack of understanding of the biblical content by those who promote and accept the principles of psychology. If this is the case, it is merely evidence of the failure to grapple with and seek the Lord for an understanding of his Word.

While I am not against psychology as a legitimate discipline studying the cause and effect of human behavior, I accept the second possibility. I believe that the presence of secular psychology within the church is filling a "lack of understanding" of the very essence of the Christian faith, which is a relationship with the person of Jesus Christ.

It is only fair to point out that it is far easier to borrow from psychology than it is to grapple with the theology of the New Testament, especially with the apostle Paul. What God offers in Christ Jesus, according to the apostle, is a mystery. Offering psychology is the easy way out. Most of the books I have read that have been written by "Christian psychologists" demonstrate a very shallow understanding of biblical theology.

I realize that in making that statement I am opening myself up to the countercriticism that what I am writing demonstrates a shallow understanding of secular psychology. I am more than willing to accept that criticism. I am not a psychologist nor have any desire to be one. I am a Christian pastor, trained in theology, who preaches Jesus Christ.

Someone might ask the legitimate question, "With a background in theology, what right do you have to assess the offerings of modern psychology?" I would answer by saying, "I have as much right as those trained in psychology do in assessing biblical theology."

Even though I will be discussing some of the offerings of modern psychology, this is not a book about psychology. It is a book about Jesus. Hopefully it will in some small way help put to rest the idea that, as far as this generation is concerned, biblical Christianity is irrelevant and will soon be replaced by modern psychology. It is my purpose to demonstrate that a relationship with the person of Jesus Christ more than adequately solves the identity crisis of this generation and brings meaning and fulfillment to life.

My primary source is the Bible, especially the epistles of the apostle Paul. Secondarily, I have borrowed a great deal from Martin Luther's understanding of Paul's teachings. Thirdly, to a limited degree, I will be offering the confirming testimony of other theologians, counselors, psychiatrists, and philosophers. Many of the concepts that I will be sharing with you do have some deep roots in theology and philosophy. To maintain a simple, readable work, I have not included some of my research in the body of the text. For those who wish to dig deeper and review the various sources for the subject matter, I have included some endnotes together with some additional commentary and explanation.

There are many who have helped me in preparing this manuscript. I especially want to thank Dr. George

Wollenburg for his many helpful insights. Dr. Francis Rossow, Pastors David Marth, Steven Cluver, and Ray Schiefelbein offered good suggestions relating to the organizing and editing of the book. A very special thanks to Eileen Mason and Bill Jensen at Harvest House for their support, encouragement, and skillful direction. May God bless your reading.

—Pastor Donald G. Matzat
St. Louis, Missouri

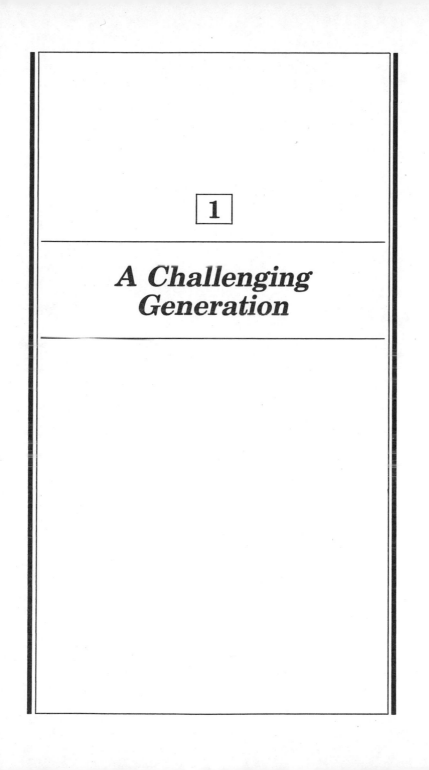

1

A Challenging Generation

*"As the struggle
for survival has subsided,
the question has emerged:
survival for what?"*
—Dr. Viktor Frankl

"Who am I?" "What is my personal identity?" "How can I develop a more positive self-image?" "Why don't I feel good about myself?" I am sure that all of you have heard these questions before. If you haven't, somehow you have been out of step with the thinking of this generation. People today are claiming that they are trying to find themselves, and need to discover who they are. We are living in an age characterized by increased self-awareness and the expansion of human consciousness. This generation is facing an identity crisis.

The needs and desires expressed by people today were generally unheard of 40 years ago. My mom, for example, who had a seventh grade education, was not concerned with her self-image. She was a housewife. I never heard her say, "I don't feel very good about myself today." My dad went to work every day. He provided for his family. He spent his evenings in front of the television and weekends "fixing up" around the house. He never raised the questions: "Who am I? What is my personal identity?" As a Christian family, we went to church every Sunday. We heard the good news that Jesus had died for our sins and that we would go to heaven when we die. All our basic needs, as we perceived them, were being met. Life in those days was quite simple.

What has happened to produce such a drastic change in the expressed needs of people?

Social Revolution

In his classic work *The Closing of the American Mind,* Dr. Allan Bloom explains the reason for the self-centered stance of most students on college campuses by saying:

> This turning in on themselves is not, as some would have it, a return to normalcy after the hectic fever of the sixties.... It is a new degree of isolation which leaves young people with no alternative to looking inward.... Country, religion, family, ideas of civilization, all the sentimental and historical forces,... *providing some notion of a place within the whole, have been rationalized and have lost their compelling force*[1] [emphasis mine].

The self-centered emphasis of this age was not merely adopted by our society as a nice way of thinking. A group of people did not put their heads together one day and decide to form a "me-generation." What has happened to people today is the result of the social dynamics of the past 30 years.

We are living in a generation that has passed through an era of profound social revolution. The civil rights movement, assassinations, Vietnam, Watergate, the population explosion, the energy shortage, "the bomb," and the sexual revolution produced a devastating adjustment in the societal mind-set. Many severed themselves from the "institution" and became free. This is a "stripped-down" generation which turned its back upon its racial distinctions, ethnic pride, national loyalty, church identity, and commitment to parental beliefs and moral values. In the words of one of the classic songs of the seventies: "Freedom's just another word for nothing left to lose."

For example, I am a white German-American from New York, a member of the Lutheran Church-Missouri Synod. Some years ago, this was my personal identity. I felt good about myself because I felt good about my national, ethnic, social, and religious connections. I was taught that my identity was the very best identity. I believed that being white was "better" than being non-white. Being German meant that I was a part of a hardworking, responsible people. As an American from New York, I lived in the very best country in the largest city. Being a member of the Lutheran Church-Missouri Synod made me a part of what my family believed to be the one, true, visible church on earth. My father referred to those who had no religious affiliation as being "nothing." While my identity was based upon stereotypes, pride, and prejudice, at least I knew who I was and felt good about myself.

But look what happened to me. I lived through and participated in the civil rights movement. I witnessed Watergate and watched our nation disintegrate over Vietnam. Television specials brought to me "Roots" and "Holocaust," causing me to jokingly comment, "It is not good being a white German." My church denomination, which had been one large, ethnic family of three million people, divided over a bloody conservative versus liberal battle. Archie Bunker prompted me to laugh at myself and at my traditional family attitudes and values.

Should I not ask the questions: "Who am I? What is my personal identity? Where is my self-worth?" Can you condemn me if I should concentrate upon trying to find myself? It is not surprising that we are living in an age of self-indulgence. Having been stripped of his previous identity, modern man discovers that all he has left is to focus upon himself.

Disillusioned

If a person rejects his identity in order to embrace the vision of a social revolution and, as a result, discovers a new and better way of life, there is no loss, but a worthwhile exchange of the lesser for the greater. For those who were committed to the revolution of the sixties and seventies, this has not been the case. Many were willing to turn away from "the institution" but received nothing in return. The dreams of a great society have vanished. Our children never heard of Woodstock, and for good reason. What did it accomplish? Abie Hoffman committed suicide. John Lennon, who "imagined" a utopian society free of man-made divisions, was shot to death. Jane Fonda has apologized to the Vietnam vets for her reaction to their war effort, and of all things, Hugh Heffner got married. In the light of the present mentality, we might conclude that Archie Bunker was right all along, and that his son-in-law "Meathead" was properly named.

It seems that there is little left to truly capture the imagination of this generation. The wrenching social concerns which challenged the youth of the sixties are but a memory. Present political issues are boring. While the exploration of outer space provides a new frontier, everyone knows there is nothing out there but emptiness.

Self-Centered

Those who left behind their former identity and received nothing in return are left without any vision for the future. They are placed into the position of focusing upon themselves. They become selfish and introverted and place their personal needs above the greater needs of society. Even their "do goodism" is often motivated by the selfish desire to feel good about themselves. A popular comic hosting a TV fund-raiser for the homeless urged contributions by saying, "Help those who are less fortunate, and you will feel so good about yourself."

By turning in on themselves, many people are confronted with the emptiness and meaninglessness of their own existence. In order to escape, they go in search of a new life. They claim that they are trying to find themselves and discover their personal identity. They change jobs and move to another city. They change marriages. They become caught up in trendy self-help therapies and methods. They adjust their styles of living; attempt to build the body beautiful; go on a diet; take up golf, tennis, or jogging; go back to school and get another degree; buy a new car or get a new hairdo. But nothing works. They cannot escape from the emptiness of their own lives. Blaise Pascal once wrote:

> The need to escape explains why many people are miserable when they are not preoccupied with work or amusements or vice. They are afraid to be alone, lest they get a glimpse of their own emptiness. When a man is left with nothing but himself to face, he falls usually into boredom, melancholy, or despair.[2]

While modern man wants to believe that he is a good, worthwhile, valuable human being, he cannot escape the emptiness and meaninglessness of his own existence. In spite of all the self-help books and the media blitz attempting to convince him that he should feel good about himself and maintain a positive image of himself, our society is faced with an epidemic of drugs, alcohol, and suicide.

Prominent psychiatrist Dr. Viktor Frankl discerned this same sense of emptiness in the lives of people who are not preoccupied with daily activities. He speaks of it as the "Sunday neurosis." He writes:

> Vast numbers of human beings,... hard at work all week long, on Sundays are overwhelmed by the emptiness and lack of content of their lives, which the day of idleness brings into consciousness. Victims of "Sunday neurosis," they get drunk in order to flee from their spiritual horror of emptiness.[3]

In assessing the feelings of this generation, Frankl writes: "The truth is that as the *struggle for survival* has subsided, the question has emerged: *survival for what?*"[4]

Meeting The Needs

This drastic change in the expressed needs of people today has had a devastating effect upon the life and influence of the traditional Christian church. The pews in many churches are occupied by senior citizens who recall the glory days of their congregation and cannot understand why "young people" no longer go to church. This is a cause for great concern, especially among those of us who are pastors in the church. It seems that people are saying to us, "We don't need you anymore." It appears, at least on the surface, that the fundamental Christian message is no longer relevant to this age.

Since many feel that traditional Christianity is unable to meet their personal needs, a vacuum is created which is filled by the teachings of modern psychology. For this reason, the influence of psychology has widely expanded, even into the church. Dr. Carl Jung stated over 50 years ago that "spiritual need has produced in our time our 'discovery' of psychology."[5]

The popular branch of psychology which is used in most counseling methods is called "humanistic psychology."

Dr. Abraham Maslow defined it as the "third force." It began as a reaction against the dehumanizing emphases of Freudianism and behaviorism. The basic idea behind humanistic psychology is that each individual person is responsible and is able to take control of his own life. He is able to find himself and feel good about himself. Out of humanist psychology have come the very popular concepts of personal identity, positive self-image, self-actualization, self-esteem, and self-worth.

While gospel preachers and teachers are viewed as merely condemning the sins of society, humanistic psychologists and counselors manifest a compassionate heart for hurting people. Many of the bestselling Christian books today are not written by Bible teachers and theologians but by Christian psychologists. This compassionate stance of psychology is not reserved only for "Christian" counselors. I know a woman who works at the counseling center at a large university. In describing the staff, she said, "These are some of the most loving, kind, compassionate people I have ever met, yet, they are all atheists."

There are many religion experts today who have written off traditional Christianity, claiming that we have nothing to say to modern man. They tell us that our theology is outdated, our message is irrelevant, and our solutions are simplistic. It has even been suggested that we are living in a "post-Christian era." Are these claims true? Should every Christian pastor have a degree in psychology if he has any hopes of reaching hurting people? How are we to respond to this present dilemma? The fields are ripe for harvest! There are many hurting people in our society who are looking for answers. Martin Luther said, "Hunger is the best cook." The problem is, how do we do it?

2

An Irrelevant Gospel?

*"The most important question
facing the church is:
'What are the deepest needs
felt by human beings?' "*
—Robert Schuller

We cannot avoid the fact that if Christianity is to remain a viable force in our society, we must be able to meet the needs of this generation. If we are not able to meet present needs, we will remain largely irrelevant, replaced by modern psychology or by the spirituality of New Age thinking. People may still come to us for their weddings and funerals, but when it comes to meeting their present needs, they will look elsewhere. Popular television personality Dr. Robert Schuller, who still continues to fill the pews in his Crystal Cathedral, believes that the most important question facing the church is: "What are the deepest needs felt by human beings?" In his opinion, religious institutions who ignore this question will remain dying churches.[1]

Do we have an answer for those who are asking the question: "Who am I, and why am I so unhappy?"

"The Ol'-Fashioned Gospel"

When you compare the needs of this generation with the traditional "ol'-fashioned gospel" proclamation of the church, it is not difficult to understand why Christianity is considered to be irrelevant. The church is seemingly out of step with the thinking of our modern society.

For example, we proclaim the forgiveness of sins as the basic, primary message of the Christian faith. In order for this good news of forgiveness to be heard and received, it must be "set up" with the message of human sin and guilt. Today, the message of sin and guilt falls upon deaf ears. Modern humanism, which considers man himself to be the measure of all things, stands against bringing him to the knowledge of sin. We are being taught to feel good about ourselves and not accept the fact that we are poor, miserable, guilty sinners in need of forgiveness.

We also proclaim the hope of eternal life in heaven for those who have been forgiven through Jesus Christ. While the issue of life after death is always somewhat relevant because we are all going to die someday, it is not today's burning issue. Modern man is seeking meaning and purpose in life today. He wants to feel good about himself . . . today. He is not terribly excited by the prospects of "pie in the sky in the great by-and-by." Reincarnation, which offers the hope of coming back into this present world, has become a popular alternative to the notion of leaving this wicked world behind and soaring into the heavens. The research of "near-death experiences" has attempted to demonstrate that there is "light at the end of the tunnel" for everybody, not merely Christians.

Our traditional "vale of tears" description of life upon this earth offers little hope for personal fulfillment. In the past, Christians hid their deep-seated personal problems behind the traditional "It is well with my soul" facade. We maintained a "stiff upper lip" in the midst of the disappointments and discouragements of life and looked for the hope of fulfillment in the eternal glory of heaven. Right or wrong, the traditional Christian expectation for life today does not provide a great deal of hope for those who are not ashamed to say that they have lost their identity and their life upon this earth is meaningless. Traditional Christians may be tempted to respond: "Be content with the fact that your sins are forgiven and you are going to heaven when you die. What more do you want?"

We are dealing today with a generation of people who have seemingly stumped the church with a new set of questions. They are not asking, "How do I get saved from sin and go to heaven when I die?" but rather, "How do I find meaning and purpose in life today?" Rather than dealing with forgiveness and eternal life, people today are concerned with *personal identity* and the meaning of their *present existence*.

Jesus Is the Answer!

While it may be true that those who are locked into proclaiming an "ol'-fashioned gospel" have been stumped by the questions of personal identity and a meaningful life today, *the writers of the New Testament were not stumped*. A reading of the New Testament, especially the epistles of Paul, clearly demonstrates that these are not foreign issues. Similar to the people of this generation, Paul had also discarded his previous identity which had been "gain to him," but for the purpose of winning Christ Jesus. In fact, he considered his former identity to be manure compared to what he had found in Christ. Inspired by the Holy Spirit, Paul identified himself in Christ, was filled with the Holy Spirit, and seated in the heavenly places. He defined himself as being "more than a conqueror" through Christ and was able "to do all things through Christ Jesus."

The personal identity of the apostle Paul was completely immersed in the person of Jesus Christ, reigning at the right hand of the Father. As far as Paul was concerned, God provided a singular answer to all human problems: the person and work of Jesus Christ. The identity and life of the apostle Paul on this earth was the result of his relationship with Jesus. He said, "For me to live is Christ!"

Should not such a glorious identity and victorious life meet the needs of this generation? If it doesn't, we can legitimately ask, "What more do you want?" A relationship with the person of Jesus Christ, who is the living and reigning King of kings and who is present in our world through the ministry of the Holy Spirit, is the answer to the needs of this generation!

What About Jesus?

It is strange that in the midst of all the criticisms being leveled against the offerings of traditional Christianity, *you never hear anyone criticize Jesus.* I have never read a book promoting the claims of modern psychology as an alternative or addition to biblical Christianity in which the author says, *"Jesus Christ does not have all the answers."* Of course, you hear it said that the "sin and grace theology of the church is not relevant," or even, "the Bible does not have all the answers," but you never hear it said that the person of Jesus Christ is an insufficient solution to the needs of modern man.

Those who promote the integration of psychology with biblical theology have *failed to grasp the basic essence of the Christian faith.* I know that is a very serious accusation, but nonetheless, when you examine the writings of Christian psychologists, it is very evident. They speak of Christianity as a specific, limited body of religious truth addressing the subject of human behavior. For example, a popular book defining the principles involved in the integration of psychology and theology states:

Many individual Christians look to psychology for new insights that will relieve personal discomfort or despair. They hope that psychology will provide answers to *questions not specifically addressed in Christianity*[2] (emphasis mine).

Dr. Gary Collins writes in his book *Can You Trust Psychology?*:

Some human problems are not mentioned in Scripture. They are not discussed specifically, neither are there examples to show how others dealt with these issues in a way pleasing to God.[3]

According to this way of thinking, the integration of psychology with theology poses no problems. Both disciplines deal with the same subject matter of human behavior and are both dedicated to helping people live more meaningful lives. Since it is philosophically correct to say that all truth ultimately comes from God, it is therefore reasonable to suggest that psychology is able to fill up that which is lacking in the body of Christian truth. This understanding is based upon a wrong definition of the very essence of Christianity.

Contrary to the thinking of Christian psychologists, Christianity is not a religion doling out spiritual wares and adjusting them from time to time to meet user demands! Nor is the Bible a fundamentalist's textbook of psychology offering a potpourri of spiritual and psychological solutions to the needs of hurting people. When confronted with the needs of people, we do not push buttons and pop out appropriate Bible verses. We offer Jesus! Christianity is and always has been a relationship with the person of Jesus Christ who is the same yesterday, today, and forever.

This raises the question: Are there human needs and problems not specifically addressed and answered in a relationship with the living person of Jesus Christ? If such needs exist, what are they? Since the essence of Christianity is found in the person and work of Jesus Christ, any claim that the Christian faith falls short in providing answers for the needs of hurting people is in fact a criticism of the sufficiency of Jesus Christ. It is one thing to claim that the traditional message of the Christian church is not sufficient to answer the questions of modern man, but it borders on heresy to suggest that there is something insufficient about what God accomplished in and through Christ Jesus.

It is only fair to point out that Christian psychologists are products of the mind-set of the traditional Christian church. Most Christians conceive of their "religion" as a specific body of propositional rules and doctrines, rather than a relationship with the living person of Jesus Christ. It is for this reason that many Christian pastors are willing to mix the truths of Christianity with the truths of psychology. As far as they are concerned, it is not mixing "apples and oranges." Even most of the arguments leveled against the intrusion of psychology into the church have been motivated by the desire to preserve the authority of the Bible as a propositional textbook. Some have even spoken of "counseling from Scripture" as if "religious," biblical rules are somehow better than the principles of psychology.

The Christian life is neither motivated by religious rules nor able to be analyzed via psychological principles. The Christian life is a result of Christ Jesus dwelling within the life of a believer.

A New Reformation

In order for the Christian church to abandon the growing dependency upon modern psychology and be able to offer Jesus Christ as the solution to human needs, we need a fresh, enlightened, biblical revelation of who Jesus is! As the Reformation of 1517 was ignited and fueled by the enlightened discovery that Christ is our righteousness, today we need our eyes opened to the reality that, in addition to being our righteousness, Jesus Christ is also our identity, our life, our fulfillment, our pride, our hope, our peace, our joy, and our ultimate worth. While we most certainly must not discard the truth of the past, we need a new reformation that will open our eyes to the full, complete salvation that God has provided for us in Christ Jesus.

Because we may be content to "get forgiven and go to heaven" does not mean that "forgiveness and eternal life" is God's only answer for the needs of men. What it does mean is that it is *our only question.* Many Christians do not have an identity problem because they fight to retain their pride and prejudices. They may know who they are, but not because of their relationship with Jesus. They find their identity in their national loyalties, ethnic pride, moral lives, religious theology, and social connections. They maintain a brand of Christianity which answers the ultimate question of life after death but has little to say about present existence. Rather than condemning the people of this generation for not embracing their Christian values, traditional morality, and responsible lifestyle, they should examine that lifestyle in the clear light of Scripture.

While it is one thing to appreciate the past or be committed to a specific doctrinal understanding, it is something quite different to use that denominational loyalty and traditional heritage as an identity. God does not identify us as being liberals or conservatives, fundamentalists or charismatics. He does not direct us to find our life in our Founding Fathers, our Constitution, our morality and American way of life. He identifies us in Christ Jesus, and has seated us with him in the heavenly places.

Those who respond to the needs of this generation by tenaciously clinging to their politically conservative mentality and calling the church back to the thinking of the forties and fifties are not a part of the solution. They are just as much a part of the problem as those who are willing to overthrow traditional Christianity and embrace psychology. Biblical Christianity is certainly not irrelevant. It is the "traditional Christian mentality" that is irrelevant! Those who severed their connections with "the institution" are probably closer to the kingdom of God than those who have identified that kingdom as "America, baseball, Chevrolet, and apple pie."

The Proper Conditions

Reformation within the church does not occur in a vacuum. It is not a sovereign move of the Holy Spirit separated from the conditions of the day. Luther's proclamation of justification by faith was to a people who were suffering from a deep sense of sin and anguish of conscience. This generally characterized the mentality of the sixteenth century. His discovery met present needs and, as a result, the church was reformed.

While our secular society is faced with a meaningless existence, most Christians today are suffering from complacency. There are many miserable, unhappy, hurting, fearful people in the church who simply put up with their condition. They may seek pity, understanding, and compassion from the pastor and their fellow church members, but they are not looking for answers. While they find their identity in their traditional connections and live moral lives by the standards of the Ten Commandments, they lack freedom, contentment, joy, and peace. We cannot say to a secular, humanistic society that Jesus Christ is the answer to their deepest needs until he is the answer to the deepest needs and longing of those who claim to be the followers of Jesus Christ.

God sent his Son into the world as the solution to the human dilemma *as he defined* the human dilemma, not as we have defined it. Regardless of the age, it has always been the will and purpose of God for us to find our identity and life in Christ Jesus. Jesus is the answer, but we have not asked all the questions. Jesus meets human needs, but we have not viewed our needs through the eyes of God. While we may think of ourselves as good, responsible, moral, religious people, God sees us as "wretched, pitiful, poor, blind, and naked" (Revelation 3:17).

Humanistic psychology defines many human needs, but at closer examination, it is merely dealing with symptoms which require the mere application of a Band-Aid to stop the bleeding. We are told, for example, that man needs to find himself. Why is this true? How did man get lost in the first place? We are told that man's most basic need is to feel good about himself. Why? Why doesn't he naturally feel good about himself? Man needs to find meaning in life. Why? Man needs a positive self-image. Why? Why does he have to develop one? Why doesn't he have one?

In sending Jesus into this world, God did not deal merely with symptoms. He got to the very heart of the matter. While the divine solution is far more drastic, it provides far greater blessings. Humanistic psychology claims to have the answers, but God, by giving to us the person of his Son, "has a much better idea" and a far more efficient solution.

3

Knowing Yourself

*"Look for yourself
and you will find in the long run
only hatred, loneliness, despair,
rage, ruin and decay."*
—C.S. Lewis

For years I wrestled with the subject of the Christian life, but it was not a very serious struggle. It was not a life-and-death-matter. I wasn't happy with myself, but then again, I wasn't really miserable either. I was "stuck in the crack," so to speak, halfway between repentance and new life.

I knew that I was a sinner, but like many Christians born and raised in a religious family, I was not a very "bad" sinner. My sense of sin was not great enough to cause me to despair and hunger for a deepened relationship with the Lord Jesus. After reading David Wilkerson's *The Cross and the Switchblade*, I admired gang leader Nicki Cruz who came to Jesus out of a deep sense of sin and guilt and found a new life. Of course, I had my share of sins, but nothing dramatic enough to be included in the content of a bestselling book. I often thought that I could be a better Christian and a much more convincing preacher of the gospel if I had committed some deep, dark sin.

I had decided to study for the ministry at the tender age of 14 and entered my church's educational system. As the years went by, I never felt compelled to examine my commitment or calling. I was too busy having a good time away at school to take spiritual matters very seriously. I seldom attended chapel services or evening devotions. When I dropped off the treadmill in 1965, armed with a degree in theology and a call to a rural congregation in southern Indiana, it did not take long before I developed a severe identity crisis. I was actually embarrassed by the title "Reverend," because I knew in my heart that I was certainly not "worthy of reverence."

While I was not a bad enough sinner to give a startling testimony of God's amazing saving grace, I did not consider myself good enough or holy enough to be a Christian pastor. If I was an ordinary church member, I would have had no problems. I would have fit in nicely with the rest of the group. But as a pastor, I was looked to as a spiritual leader, the instructor of the youth, the guardian of the faith, and an example of Christian maturity. I was placed upon a pedestal and, as a result, felt like a phony.

I began to study the subject of the Christian life as a result of meeting some "born-againers" who continued to pester me with their testimonies of a newly found relationship with Jesus Christ. They made me feel very threatened and insecure. While I knew my stuff when it came to theology and doctrine, they claimed to know the Lord. One man, who was probably able to see through my pastoral veneer, gave me some books written by men I had never heard of before; Watchman Nee, Andrew Murray, A.W. Tozer. Out of curiosity, I read them. The material was intriguing. I was confronted with an understanding of Romans 6, 7, and 8 which I had never heard before. In addition, each of the authors possessed a depth of understanding concerning the subject of human sin.

As a means of comparison, I also read some material by Martin Luther, especially his commentaries on Romans and Galatians. I was very impressed with Luther's depth of Christian faith and life. He certainly would not have been accused of promoting a high level of human self-esteem. He wrote that man must come to *a knowledge of himself, be terrified of himself, and be crushed* as a prelude to receiving and appreciating God's grace, forgiveness, and new life in Christ Jesus.[1] I knew that Luther had not fallen into gross public sins, but somehow he knew the perverted condition of his own heart.

"Lord, Show Me My Heart"

It seemed to me that an in-depth knowledge of sin was a necessary step in Christian growth, so I began to pray that God would show me my heart. It was not the disciplined, formal, "kneel down, fold your hands and implore heaven" type of prayer, but a simple, offhanded expression, "God, I need to know my heart." I had read somewhere that God was very willing, by his Holy Spirit, to show us our sin. David had prayed in the psalms, "Search me, O Lord." I really did not expect anything to happen as a result of my informal, somewhat flippant prayer, but...

One cold November night I caught a glimpse of myself that scared the life out of me. Just a few weeks before, my wife had come home from the hospital with our third child, a beautiful, brown-eyed baby girl whom we named Susan. As is often the case with babies—and Susan was no exception—a middle-of-the-night feeding was required.

In the midst of a deep sleep, I heard the voice of my wife, "Come on, wake up! You feed her tonight. I'm tired."

"You gotta be kidding," I responded. In the background I could hear the sound of Susan wailing in the next room. "Can't you feed her? I'm tired too."

"I have been up with her every night since we came home," my wife responded somewhat angrily. "You can get up with her one night."

She was right. I had not yet participated in Susan's middle-of-the-night ritual. So I crawled out from under the warm covers.

"Brrr, it's cold..." I quietly exclaimed as my feet hit the floor. November in central Michigan is not characterized by warm nights. The clock told me it was 2:15.

I stumbled into the next room and gently picked up my little girl out of her crib and together we headed for the kitchen. As the bottle was being warmed, she continued to wail in spite of my words of assurance that the bottle would soon be ready.

Finally Daddy and his little girl sat down together on the living room sofa and the feeding began. It was a beautiful, cold, crisp night. The moonlight streaming in through the open drapes created an eerie effect. There was something nice about the moment, something nostalgic.

After the bottle had been sucked dry, we began walking the floor together, seeking that all-important burp. Finally it came. Praising Susan for the fact that she worked so well, I gently lowered her from my shoulder into my arms. We paced the floor together. While I was gently singing "Jesus loves me this I know," her eyelids grew heavy, and she went back to sleep. I was proud of my accomplishment. I was eagerly anticipating jumping back under the warm covers with a sense of satisfaction over a job well done.

Tiptoeing back down the hallway to her room, I very carefully lowered her into her crib and covered her with a blanket. She looked so beautiful, so much at peace. Gently closing her door behind me, I headed back to bed.

Just as I had pulled the warm covers around me, closed my eyes, and began to drift off, I heard the worst possible sound. Susan began to scream.

I discovered an intense anger and rage welling up within me. I quickly jumped out of bed and angrily marched down the hall to Susan's room. Just as I pushed open the door, the thought crossed my mind:

"See what kind of a person you are...." I stopped dead in my tracks. My anger subsided.

"Wow," I thought to myself as I gently lifted Susan from the crib, "I could have struck my little girl." I felt so very ashamed and even apologized to my baby for my anger. As far as I was concerned, any person who would strike a helpless infant is the ultimate lowlife. Yet, I was capable of doing such a thing. I had been on the brink of losing control, gripped by an anger and rage over the fact that my little daughter was taking away my comfort, robbing me of a few extra moments of sleep.

Thus began an eye-opening process of self-knowledge. After numerous other less-dramatic experiences, I came to the conclusion that given the right set of circumstances, I was capable of anything. I was convinced that there was no sin that I could not commit, no perverse act in which I could not participate if the conditions were right. I was afraid of myself. I no longer admired those who came to Jesus out of great despair and guilt—I knew that "but for the grace of God, there go I." For the very first time in my life, *I saw myself as God saw me: wretched, pitiful, poor, blind, and naked.* I really needed Jesus!

Sin and Grace

If you read about the experiences of Christians who progressed in their relationship with the Lord Jesus beyond the norm, you will note the combination of a deep sense of sin and failure together with a deep appreciation for what God accomplished in Christ Jesus. Men such as John Calvin, John Wesley, Martin Luther, C.S. Lewis, and Francis Schaeffer were not afraid to speak of their sinful nature and even boast of their weaknesses, because they possessed a new life in Christ. The writings of such men reflect a profound level of spiritual depth and biblical insight, causing the theology of those who are offering the solutions of modern psychology to look shallow by comparison.

In observing this reality of the relationship between sin and grace in his patients, Paul Tournier writes:

> This can be seen in history; for believers who are the most desperate about themselves are the ones who express most forcefully their confidence in grace.... Those who are the most pessimistic about man are the most optimistic about God; those who are the most severe with themselves are the ones who have the most serene confidence in divine forgiveness.... By degrees the awareness of our guilt and of God's love increase side by side.[2]

Avoiding Self-Knowledge

Arriving at an accurate self-knowledge based upon the divine assessment of our lives is a very difficult but necessary step in finding our life in Christ. If we do not know ourselves and come to grips with the depth of sin within our hearts, our relationship with Jesus will remain superficial.

Even though we might outwardly claim that we are deeply interested in spiritual knowledge and growth, it is a characteristic of our human nature to avoid getting to know ourselves because of what we might discover hidden within the depth of our hearts.[3] Our sinful pride fights against the exposure of our thoughts, intentions, motives, and desires. But without such exposure, we become easy prey to the wiles of the devil who knows our hearts and is able to exploit our weaknesses. Seventeenth-century philosopher Blaise Pascal once wrote, "Truly it is an evil to be full of faults, but it is a still greater evil ... to be unwilling to recognize them."[4]

By failing to know ourselves, unmask our pretensions, and come to grips with the reality of our corrupted human existence, we live a lie. While God says we are sinners, we want to be considered saints, so we live a charade. Our greatest fear becomes being unmasked. While our righteousness is as filthy rags, we want to be known as good people, so our lives become controlled by the opinions of others. While our pride feeds on the praise and recognition we receive for our accomplishments, we want to be known as humble and selfless, so we cannot really enjoy what we achieve lest people think we are proud.

The pursuit of self-knowledge is an endless task. We never arrive at the place of being fully aware of the depth of sin that dwells within our hearts. Soren Kierkegaard stated that each new day, we are faced with further surprises and bafflements. We are never safe and secure from the outbreaks of temptation and failure.[5]

Biblical Christianity and humanistic psychology do agree on the one basic point that we must come to a knowledge of ourselves, *but for different reasons.* While humanistic psychology teaches us to know ourselves so that we might feel good about ourselves, biblical Christianity teaches us to know ourselves so that we might turn away from ourselves and discover our life and identity in Christ Jesus.

4

The Right Diagnosis

"Lord, I see it now!
Not only what I have done is wrong;
I am wrong!"
—Watchman Nee

Christians who come to grips with the perverted condition of their sinful nature and set out on the path of self-improvement soon discover that there is something very wrong. They find that, no matter how hard they try, they are unable to change their lives. There must be literally millions of Christians who have discovered this frustration. It is a common experience.

We know that God has established in his Word some rather stringent rules for living which not only involve external actions, but also inner attitudes, reactions, intentions, motives, etc. If we resolve to conform our life to the divine standard, we will be frustrated. We may make vows and promises, only to break them. We may try to stir up greater willpower and plead with God to help, but nothing works.

When I came to realize the depth of sin within my own heart, I determined that I had to change. I knew that my sins were forgiven through the death of Jesus Christ, but I was becoming increasingly unhappy with my condition. In addition, I was also becoming increasingly disenchanted with the pastoral ministry. I was very tired of being a phony.

I certainly wanted to change, but lacked the power and ability. I found myself saying with Paul, "For I have the desire to do what is good, but I cannot carry it out" (Romans 7:18). I wanted to be more loving, gentle, and kind, but didn't know how to do it. I honestly desired to overcome the weaknesses of my sinful flesh, but continued to fail. I wanted to spend more time in prayer, but had no discipline. I desired a greater measure of peace and joy, but found myself continually faced with guilt and condemnation.

No Answers!

I believed that somewhere there had to be a solution. Like many Christians today, I went out in search for an answer.

I threw myself into a study of Christian ethics, hoping to find a system that would work. I read a great deal of material, but it didn't make a bit of difference. No matter what system I adopted, I didn't change. The problem was not intellectual.

Some authors led me on a more spiritual approach, telling me that if I read the Bible more, prayed more, and had a disciplined "quiet time" with the Lord, I would grow spiritually and change. I gave it a try. One morning I actually got up very early to pray, but fell asleep. Telling an undisciplined sinner to become disciplined is not the solution. While it is certainly God's desire for us to pray and read our Bibles, this is not a "religious exercise" nor a human good work. It is to be the spontaneous result of the Holy Spirit building us up in our relationship with Jesus. I was putting the cart before the horse. The answer was not found in more religion.

I got involved in the "encounter group" movement, believing that if I became a part of a support group and openly confessed my sins to others, I would change. I formed little sensitivity groups within my congregation and became a part of a pastor's "spill your guts and be real" group. Even though I was willing to tell people my problems, it made little difference. I did not have a psychological problem which required a psychological solution.

I became a part of the charismatic movement. I was told that I really needed to "get baptized in the Holy Spirit," speak in tongues, praise God in the midst of difficult situations, be delivered from a demon, or have some hidden, unresolved conflicts within my unconscious mind healed, but it didn't work! It was by and large a false hope. One evening I was teaching in a charismatic prayer group. I asked the 200 or so people gathered, "How many of you believed and confessed at one time that God had delivered you of a certain sin only to discover that it came back again?" As I had expected, just about every hand went up. My problem was not even a spiritual problem. No matter what I did, the old sins and failures continued to stick up their ugly heads.

I Was the Problem!

One day, in studying Romans chapters 7 and 8, my attention became riveted upon the last verses in chapter 7. The apostle Paul had cried out: "O wretched man that I am!" (KJV) I read that verse over and over again: "*Wretched* man that I am..." "Wretched *man* that I am..." "Wretched man that I *am*..." As I meditated upon those words, the thought hit me, "The apostle Paul didn't have a problem—he considered himself to be the problem."

In the entire epistle to the Romans, verse 24 of chapter 7 is a key transitional verse. It connects the frustration of the apostle in chapter 7 with his understanding of the victory in Christ Jesus revealed in chapter 8.

In between the defeat of Romans 7 and the victory of Romans 8 was the cry of despair: "O wretched man that I am." While all Christians experience the frustration of Romans 7, few are willing to arrive at the conclusion to Romans 7. For this reason, they neither understand nor experience the victorious cry of the apostle in Romans 8, "I am more than a conqueror!"

I am sure that Paul did not arrive at his "O wretched man that I am" conclusion without a great struggle. He had every reason to fight for his dignity. He was a Pharisee and probably used every remembrance of the performance of his self-righteous religious duties for his self-preservation. Finally he yielded to the truth revealed to him by the Holy Spirit and declared, "I am a wretch!" In Philippians 3:4-7, he wrote:

> If anyone else thinks he has reasons to put confidence in the flesh, I have more: circumcised on the eighth day, of the people of Israel, of the tribe of Benjamin, a Hebrew of Hebrews, in regard to the law, a Pharisee; as for zeal, persecuting the church; as for legalistic righteousness, faultless. But whatever was to my profit I now consider loss for the sake of Christ.

He evaluated the entire content of his former identity by saying, "But what things were gain to me . . . I . . . do count them but dung that I may win Christ!" (Philippians 3:7,8 KJV)

Wretch! Dung! Manure! Can you imagine a person coming to the point in his life when he assesses his entire former identity and regards himself as a wretch and the content of his life as being manure? What a devastating experience! This was the experience of the apostle Paul.

What really grabbed my attention was the fact that he did not discard his former identity because he had something else going for him. He was not joining a social revolution in order to build some utopian heaven on earth. He was not shifting from "liberal" Judaism to "conservative" Christianity. He was not seeking a greater personal "holiness" than that which he had as a Pharisee. He did not discard the past in order to gain a "deeper spirituality" or a higher position in the church. He was not passing through a mid-life identity crisis in which he rejected his former identity in order to discover a new "self." He rejected and rebuked his former identity, evaluated it as manure, "in order to win Christ." He was *pursuing the person of Jesus Christ.*

As a result of studying the experience of the apostle Paul, I discovered the answer to my problem. I did not like the answer very much, but it became very clear that I did not have a problem. Rather, I *was* the problem, and *Jesus was the solution!*

In his classic work titled *The Normal Christian Life,* Watchman Nee precisely described my experience when he wrote:

> At the beginning of our Christian life we are concerned with our doing, not with our being; we are distressed rather by what we have done than by what we are. We think that if only we could rectify certain things we should be good Christians, and we set out therefore to change our actions. . . . The more we try to rectify matters on the outside the more we realize how deep-seated is the trouble. Then we come to the Lord and say, "Lord, I see it now! Not only what I have *done* is wrong; *I* am wrong."[1]

Arriving at this position simplified the entire issue of the Christian life. I did not feel good about myself, because I wasn't supposed to. I didn't have a negative self-image; I had a negative self. As an old joke put it: "He didn't have an inferiority complex. He was simply inferior."

All the frustration that is experienced by those who search for a changed life and victory over sin is based on a wrong diagnosis of the human condition. We erroneously believe that God is in the repair business, that he compassionately repairs human lives like a friendly father fixing his children's broken toys. We make up a list of our specific problems and go about seeking the Lord for specific solutions, but nothing ever gets checked off the list and it seemingly never ends.

I heard a Christian counselor say, "The Bible raises many questions about human behavior, but has no answers." He is right! The Bible does not provide specific solutions for specific human behavioral problems. God does not repair and adjust human life. From his perspective, human life is beyond repair.

Against the Tide...

I do not have to tell you that considering yourself to be a "wretch" and evaluating the content of your life as "manure" goes against the tide of popular thinking that is in the church today. Many Christians, pastors, church leaders, and seminary instructors have embraced the understanding of humanistic psychology and teach people to feel good about themselves. My position would be considered an insult to human dignity. In fact, some churches have foolishly removed words such as "wretch," "worm," and "worthless" from their hymnody because they believe that using such terms will merely produce negative behavior.

If in searching for an answer to my problem I would have entered therapy and come under the influence of a humanistic counselor rather than reading and studying the inspired words of the apostle Paul, I would have been told that my problem is not what I am, but rather what I think I am. I would have been diagnosed as lacking a due sense of self-esteem and self-worth. I would have been told that I should not be referring to myself as a "wretch." Rather, I should believe and confess that I am a valuable, worthwhile human being. Of course, if I had arrived at that conclusion, I would not have needed Jesus.

My human pride does not like the Bible's solution to my problem. I would prefer to have a Father in heaven who would lift me on to his lap, solve all my little problems and failures, assure me that I am a fine person, pat me on the rump, and send me on my way. In this way I could preserve my dignity and be a good Christian, but I would never realize how much I need Jesus. I could "have my cake and eat it too." But this is not God's way of dealing with the human condition. God tells me that I am the problem, and his Son is the solution.

When people come to me for help in dealing with their problems in life, I do not relish offering the Bible's assessment of their situation. It causes me to appear insensitive to human needs. I would much prefer telling people that they are good, valuable, worthwhile human beings. This would also help my self-esteem, because they would like me. Not too many "compassionate" Christian psychologists would have the nerve to listen to a person sharing all her problems and heartaches and respond by saying, "My dear, you don't have a problem. You *are* the problem!" Offering such a solution would not increase "counseling business." This is probably the last thing people want to hear, and they certainly wouldn't pay good money to hear it! I thank God that he loves us enough to tell us the truth!

A Scientific Solution?

The claim is made that humanistic psychology offers a "scientific" solution to the human dilemma based upon observable data. What about the biblical solution? Is it scientific? Does it agree with observable facts?

If you evaluate the biblical diagnosis of the human dilemma by objectively comparing it with your own life experiences, you will discover that it is completely in line with reality. For example, I had always blamed other people, circumstances, and situations beyond my control for my unhappiness. "If I could change the circumstances," I reasoned, "I could be happy." But into each situation I entered, there was a singular constant: ME! While my situations, circumstances, and relationships with other people were always changing, I remained the same.

If I was not happy no matter what was happening around me, obviously, I had to be the problem. Based on very clear scientifically verifiable evidence observed over many years of personal experience, I was and continue to be the problem!

Fighting the Truth

Everything within our fallen human nature resists the divine assessment of the human dilemma. It is amazing how we fight to hang on to the tattered garments of our own righteousness and struggle to preserve our last scrap of human dignity. Even in situations where we pass through times of great turmoil and deeply experience the guilt and despair of our own human sin and failure and have our pride "worked over" by the circumstances of life, we refuse to admit that we are the problem. While everyone else around us realizes that we are at fault, we claim that we are either the victims of circumstances or casualties resulting from the unfair, immoral actions of other people. We seek to justify ourselves!

For a number of years I counseled off and on with a young woman who had a multitude of problems. Because I knew some of the devastating experiences that had been a part of her childhood, I avoided accusing her of wrong until she was ready to hear it. While her first two marriages ended in divorce, her third marriage ended as a result of the death of her husband in an automobile accident. Viewing herself as a victim of circumstances, she began carousing through the bars, being willing to sleep with anyone who offered her love and affection.

One day she came to talk to me. She was very frantic and hysterical. It seemed that her parents and her former in-laws had rejected her and wanted nothing to do with her, accusing her of being a prostitute. This produced within her much grief and guilt. By her own admission, she had hit the bottom and could get no lower. At the risk of being considered insensitive, but with the hope of sharing with her the good news of a relationship with the Lord Jesus, I gently suggested that she was not a victim of circumstances and that perhaps she should recognize that she is the source of her own problems and come to an end of her own efforts and accept Jesus.

As I began to explain to her the basics of the gospel, her countenance changed. She stopped crying. Her face hardened. She lit up a cigarette and adamantly declared: "I'm not ready for that yet!" She angrily got up and left. I never saw her again.

Like so many, she was not interested in the truth. She was merely seeking justification for her actions and confirmation of her opinion that the real problem was with her parents and in-laws. As long as I was willing to affirm her and provide support for her own self justification, I was her friend who was being sensitive to her needs. But when I came to the place of loving her enough to speak the truth, she was not interested.

Why Me?

The Word of God does not tell us that "we are the problem" merely to make us feel bad about ourselves or to blame ourselves. God deals with reality—not with emotions, feelings, and human opinions. To consider yourself to be a poor, miserable, perverted sinner is not merely manifesting some self-effacing, humble attitude.

We are the problem because of our identity, because of who we are. When we find ourselves, we have discovered the problem. As the comic strip character Pogo put it, "We have met the enemy, and it is us."

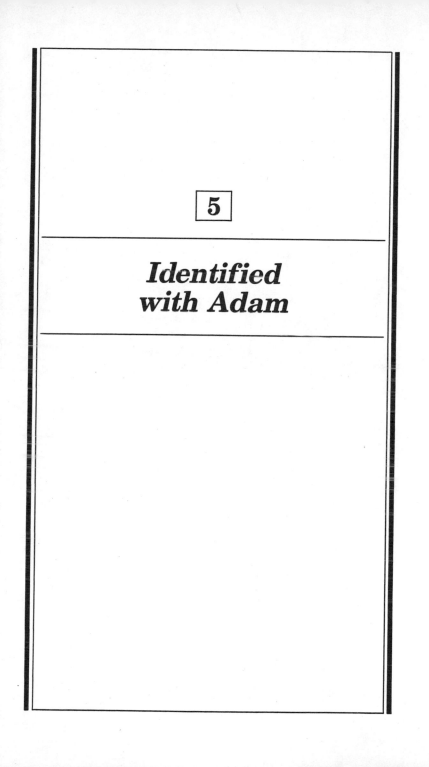

5

Identified with Adam

"As in Adam all men die..."
—St. Paul

How we reflect upon our "self" is called our self-image. On the basis of the content of the previous chapter, it might be suggested that I possess a very negative self-image. For me to speak of myself as a "wretch," define the content of my life as "manure," and see myself as the cause of my problems would lead to the conclusion that I do not feel very good about my "self."

My position toward "self" is hardly the result of an emotional "poor me" attitude. If this were the case, I certainly would not be boasting of my weaknesses in the public forum. I do not walk around from day to day with my head down and groan, "Woe is me, I am such a wretch." I am not asking you to feel sorry for me. My "negative self-image" is beyond emotion and is based upon some very cold, historical facts.

When I speak about my "self," I am not talking about some mysterious essence hidden deep within the vague parameters of my alleged unconscious mind, nor am I referring to my eternal soul. These are some of the definitions of "self" used in segments of modern psychology. I use the term "self" to define my human life, my personality, everything about me that is able to be revealed and evaluated: my will, desires, intentions, and goals; my intellect, words, and thoughts; my emotions, feelings, attitudes, and reactions.[1] When I speak about "self," I am simply referring to the content of my life. A self-image defines the manner in which we judge and evaluate our lives.

Our self-image is very important. It has been said that the teaching regarding self-image is the most important psychological discovery of this century.[2] If we do not have a self-image, we cannot answer the question "Who am I?" We have no way of making an accurate identification. The person who does not know himself or cannot find himself does not possess a self-image.

We are only able to identify an object because we have a mental image of how the object was originally identified. For example, I look at an object on my desk and say, "That is a lamp." How do I know that it is a lamp? Simply, because I know how to identify a lamp. By comparing the object on my desk with the original "lamp-image" in my mind, I am able to make an identification. Without a "self-image" I have no way of identifying "self."

It is difficult to change the original mental image that we have of various objects. For example, many years ago the large box containing chunks of ice that was kept in the kitchen in order to keep food cool was called an "ice box." Today, we no longer have "ice boxes," we have electric refrigerators. Yet, many people, when referring to the large box in the kitchen, still speak of the "ice box." It was the original identity of the box.

Those who teach the principles of modern psychology believe that we must develop a positive self-image. We must feel good about ourselves. They claim that many of our behavioral problems are caused by a negative self-image which we formed from the opinions of other people—such as parents and teachers—who told us that we were not good people. If our behavior is to be adjusted, we must begin by developing a new, positive image of ourselves based upon positive opinions. How is this done?

We develop this new self-image by creating in our mind a positive picture of who we are. We then identify our true selves in that positive picture and thereby answer the question "Who am I?" We find ourselves in our own manufactured self-image. When you think about it, this is really a fascinating game. We make up our own rules, set the standards, associate with those who agree with us, and pat ourselves on the back for playing the game so well. It seems to me that the game is "fixed."

The Bible, on the other hand, doesn't play games. We are given a very clear way of answering the question "Who am I?" The Bible gives to us a picture of our original identification. We find ourselves in the original, "in Adam." The Bible identifies us with Adam. When we look at Adam, we know who we are. The Hebrew word "adam" means "man."

"In Adam"

The Bible identifies the entire human race "in Adam." In 1 Corinthians 15:22, we read: "For as in Adam all die." Everyone who is a part of the human race is born from Adam's life and is a sinner, destined to die. Paul writes: "Sin entered the world through one man, and death through sin" (Romans 5:12). This is an objective reality which accurately defines the human condition.

We are not sinners because we sin. We are sinners because we were born out of the wrong root—the root of Adam. When Adam sinned, we became sinners. This became our personal identity. There is an old German hymn which is titled, "Durch Adams Fall ist ganz verderbt." Translated that means, "Through Adam's fall is everything destroyed."

Being "in Adam" means that Adam's nature determined our identity in the same manner that our parents' race, nationality, and perhaps religion, politics, and economic and social standing determined our "immediate" identity. While we may attempt to reject most of the identity handed down by our parents, there are certain things we are stuck with. We cannot change our race or national origin, and of course, we are always stuck with Adam. We are in him and cannot get out of him until the day we leave him in the dust from whence he came.

We may try to "get out of Adam" by claiming that he was not a historical person and adopt evolution as our theory of human origin. This really wreaks havoc with our personal identity. It is one thing to turn to Genesis and find our original identity in Adam; it is another thing to go to the zoo and find our original identity in the primate cage.

"Adam Is in Us"

When we were born into this world, not only were we born "in Adam" or out of the root of Adam, but the rebellious nature of Adam also was born in us. We became sinners by experience. The full content of Adam's perverted nature was joined and cemented to us. Sin became our experience. Therefore, we are sinners "objectively" because we were born out of the root of Adam, and we are sinners "subjectively" because the old nature of Adam is joined to us. Our identity or position is that of being a sinner. Our life and experience is also that of being a sinner. In this one sense, humanistic psychology is correct in saying that our personal identity determines our actions. Because we are identified in and with Adam, we are sinners; therefore, we sin. I am not a sinner because I sin. I sin because I am a sinner.

This truth is certainly not hard to demonstrate. If you keep your eye on any little "innocent" baby that is born into this world, you will discover that the "sweet little thing" turns into a selfish, disobedient "monster" at about the age of two. He manifests his real identity. This can be very embarrassing, especially if the parents were proud of and defended their personal identity created by a manufactured self-image. Their offspring demonstrate beyond any doubt that Mom and Dad were operating under a false identity. I could dress up my dog as a little girl and identify her as such, but as soon as she gives birth to barking pups, I become quite certain that I made a wrong identification. If parents want to preserve their public self-image, they have to keep their kids in the house.

We Have Sinned!

Because we have been born out of the root of Adam, we have sinned and fallen short of the glory of God. We have not done the things God has commanded us to do, nor have we avoided the things he has commanded us not to do. Even though we seek to live moral, responsible lives and may do a fairly good job of it, our hearts are wrong. Our attitudes do not reflect the love, joy, and peace which God desires for us. Our intentions and motives are primarily self-centered. Because of our pride, we are quick to break relationships and hold back forgiveness from others. Because our lives are wrapped up in ourselves, we worry about our future and fear sickness, tragedy, or death. We feel sorry for ourselves. In order to make ourselves look good in the eyes of others, we readily judge those who do not live up to our standards. If we do not get our way, we become angry and resentful. Putting it very simply, our lives are a mess!

The Bible is very clear in its estimate of human life. We are the children of wrath (Ephesians 2:3), totally unable by nature to grasp the things of the Spirit of God

(1 Corinthians 2:14). The Bible tells us that we were shaped in iniquity and born in sin (Psalm 51:5), and that the imaginations of our hearts are evil (Genesis 8:21). Within our human flesh, there dwells absolutely no good thing. Even though we may desire to do good and to be good, we are unable to accomplish our lofty ideals because our nature is wrong (Romans 7:18,19). We are in bondage to the law of sin and death (Romans 7:21).

The Blessings of Adam

Because we have been born out of the root of Adam, we have other "human" characteristics which we inherited from Adam. We have been "richly blessed" by Adam with many interesting traits.

Why is it, for example, that we refuse to accept blame and are always "passing the buck" to other people? While every Christian is theoretically willing to say, "I am a sinner, and I have fallen short of God's glory," when "push comes to shove" over placing blame for specific incidents of sin and wrongdoing, the same self-confessed sinner will try every means possible to avoid having the finger of accusation pointed at him. "Self" will be defended at all costs.

The need to justify ourselves is a very normal human response. If you live in a family with more than one child, determining which child is responsible for a misdeed is often impossible. There are times when parents are convinced that things get broken, food gets eaten, rooms get messed, and walls get dirtied and no one is responsible. As Bill Cosby declares, "Having one child is easy. If something gets broken, you know who did it."

Self-justification and the avoidance of guilt is not reserved for children only. We never outgrow the need to justify our actions before others so that we will appear to be in the right and thereby preserve our dignity. While we are very quick to pass judgement upon the actions of other people, if a judgment is leveled against us we will seek ways and means and devise various schemes to defend ourselves, even though in our hearts we know that we were wrong. I am sure that all of you have been in situations in which you have contrived some rather farfetched explanations to defend your questionable behavior. In describing the roots of self-justification, Dr. Paul Tournier wrote in his book *Guilt and Grace*:

> In a healthy person... this defense mechanism has the precision and universality of a law of nature.... We defend ourselves against criticism with the same energy we employ in defending ourselves against hunger, cold or wild beasts, for it is a moral threat.[3]

Why is the desire for self-justification a common human characteristic? While psychologists might understand what self-justification is and how it works, they don't know why it is a part of human behavior. To answer the question, we have to look at Adam.

Adam and Eve knew that they had sinned. Their guilt even drove them into hiding. They knew their condition. But what happens when God levels the finger of accusation?

"It's not my fault," cries Adam. "It was that woman that you gave me."

"It's not my fault," Eve protests, "It was that snake that you created and left roaming around the garden."

While they both knew very well that they had sinned and disobeyed God, they were unwilling to accept the blame. In fact, in their eyes God was the one who was ultimately responsible for the misdeed. This attitude of Adam is clearly identified in us!

Consider another interesting characteristic: Why are we so wrapped up in ourselves? Why are we so self-conscious and afraid of what other people are thinking of us? How did we get to be self-conscious? Animals do not appear to be self-conscious. I don't believe that my dog actually knows that he exists. He is certainly not very concerned by what the other dogs in the neighborhood think of him. How did we get to be so self-conscious? Again, look at Adam!

There is good evidence to suggest that Adam was not self-conscious prior to his falling into sin. While the Bible does not specifically make that statement, the content of the Genesis account—together with the call of the gospel away from "self" and unto Jesus—leads to that conclusion.[4] There is no doubt that Adam was aware of his own existence in his relationship with God, with Eve, and with the whole creation, but the question directed to him by God, "Who told you that you were naked? Have you eaten from the tree that I commanded you not to eat from?" (Genesis 3:11) indicates that Adam may have had no self-awareness prior to falling into sin. His consciousness was directed at his Creator. He therefore lived in harmony with Eve and with the whole creation. The Lord God was asking, "Adam, why are you looking at yourself and judging yourself?"

Perhaps C.S. Lewis is providing us with an accurate description of the nature of the fall of man into sin in his science-fiction novel *Perelandra*. In depicting the lives of a man and woman living on another planet untainted by sin, he portrays the devil as tempting the woman by providing her with a mirror so that she was able to reflect upon herself.

Finding Yourself in Adam

While it is certainly true that Adam was originally created in the "image of God," which meant that he found himself by looking at God, when he fell into sin he took his eyes off God and focused upon himself. In this way, he became lost. He chose to separate himself from the source of his identity: his God. It is no wonder that modern man is looking for himself. "Being lost" is also a characteristic of Adam.

In answer to the question "Who am I?", the Bible directs us back to the original man. We discover our personal identity in Adam. We do not get to know ourselves by listening to the opinions of other people. Whether the opinions are positive or negative makes absolutely no difference. We identify ourselves as we would identify any object: in the original image or mental picture of the object. God provides such an image by directing us to Adam. Only when I find myself in Adam, have I really found myself. I might not like my discovery; nonetheless, it is the real me.

Recognizing that we are born in Adam and that our personal identity and self-image are found in the rebellious nature of Adam is not intended to produce in us an emotional, "poor me" attitude. To feel sorry for ourselves because we were born with a corrupted human nature and are therefore the cause of our own problems is silliness. Our condition is based upon cold, historical facts that we cannot avoid! The question is, what are we going to do about it?

6

Turning Away from Self

*"If one died for all, then are
all dead."*
—St. Paul

If I am the problem, what is the solution? If you educate me, you will get a smart sinner. If you discipline me, you will get a disciplined sinner. If you refine me, I becomed a refined sinner. If you give me more religion, I will be a religious sinner. Whatever you do with me, you cannot change what I am, and what I am is the problem.

Contrary to popular opinion, how I think about myself will not change the situation nor adjust what I am. Embracing a positive image of self will not, in the long run, make any difference, because I am still wrapped up in myself. I simply become a self-centered sinner who is trying to like himself. Even if I feel bad about myself and do not like myself, I am still focusing upon myself, and "myself" is the problem. The corrupted condition of my human "self" is not a mere figment of imagination which can be adjusted by thinking differently.

The real issue before us is *the focus upon self and the consciousness of self itself.* It is certainly not the purpose and will of God for us to be concentrated upon ourselves. I would challenge anyone to demonstrate where the Bible teaches us to be consciously concerned with our self-image. Urging Christians to become engrossed in self by seeking to develop self-esteem is not a part of the solution to the human dilemma. Since I am the problem, focusing attention upon myself merely magnifies, activates, and compounds the problem. Jesus tells us to deny ourselves. Such self-denial is not the giving up of ice cream for Lent but is the actual denial of "self" itself.

A popular advocate of the positive self-image teaching wrote, "What you think of yourself influences every part of your life."[1]

It is far more biblically correct to say, "*That* you think of yourself influences every part of your life"! We could even say, "*When* you are thinking of yourself, every part of your life is being negatively influenced." The real question is: "*Why* are you thinking about yourself?"

The call of the gospel is away from self and unto Jesus, because *self is the problem and Jesus is the solution.* The apostle Paul admonishes: "And he died for all, that those who live should no longer live for themselves but for him who died for them and was raised again" (2 Corinthians 5:15). In his classic work *Mere Christianity,* C.S. Lewis wrote:

> But there must be a real giving up of the self. You must throw it away "blindly" so to speak. Christ will indeed give you a real personality: but you must not go to Him for the sake of that. As long as your own personality is what you are bothering about, you are not going to Him at all. The very first step is to try to forget about the self altogether.[2]

"No longer live for yourself"? "Throw 'self' away blindly"? "Forgetting about self altogether"? These are radical statements, especially in this age of self-esteem. What does it mean to get away from yourself, and how can we accomplish it? Am I suggesting a personal nihilism which negates the reality of human existence? Are we talking about a denial of our problems, or a repression of our inner conflicts? Are we actually capable of getting away from ourselves or leaving ourselves behind, or is it merely a futile attempt, similar to trying to lose our own shadow?

Before we discuss the clear biblical basis for "getting off self" and "throwing self away blindly," let us first consider this subject from a purely human, psychological perspective. Since the entire self-esteem, positive-self-image teaching is a product of modern humanistic psychology, consider what another "expert" in the field of human behavior has to say about "getting away from self."

Self-Detachment

According to the theories of human behavior proposed by the noted Viennese psychiatrist Dr. Viktor Frankl, the father of *logotherapy,* "getting off self" is well within our capability. While Frankl's theories certainly do not offer any lasting solutions for human problems, he is one of the few theorists within humanistic psychology who accurately identifies one aspect of the problem. While most teach self-esteem and urge us to reflect positively upon ourselves, Viktor Frankl calls us to forget about ourselves. He teaches self-detachment.

Dr. Frankl uses the principle of "self-detachment" as the foundation for his *logotherapy* approach to helping people work through their personal problems. He urges those who are burdened by the meaninglessness of their daily lives to separate from themselves and become involved in other activities or develop relationships with other people. Frankl speaks of this action of getting away from self as a "coping mechanism built into the human psyche."[3]

His understanding and application of the concept of self-detachment is based upon his experiences in the death camps of Auschwitz where he was held captive during the Second World War. He noticed that those who maintained their mental and emotional stability in the midst of the horrible conditions of a concentration camp had detached themselves from themselves and had become engrossed in other activities and relationships. Frankl points out that the more one forgets oneself—giving oneself to a cause or another person—the more human he is. He says, "The more one is immersed and absorbed in something or someone other than oneself, the more he really becomes human."[4] According to Dr. Viktor Frankl, a noted specialist in human behavior, separating from self and throwing self away is within human capacity. We are not stuck with self. Frankl writes, "Human freedom implies man's capacity to detach himself from himself."[5] On the basis of his understanding, we are not suggesting the psychologically damaging attitudes of nihilism, or the repression and denial of our problems, inner hurts, and conflicts. What we are saying is that focusing upon these things neither solves them nor changes them but merely magnifies and activates them.

The Proper Response to the Cross

For the Christian, "getting off self'" is more than merely a "coping mechanism built into the human psyche." Nor is turning away from self a technique or gimmick to make us feel better. It is our only proper response to what God has accomplished in Christ Jesus.

Every stance that a Christian occupies toward self and toward God is motivated by the Holy Spirit working through the revealed Word of God, producing a faith response. I am not offering a psychological mechanism for dealing with the problems of life which has been discovered as the result of observation or the often conflicting results of "scientific" testing. I am talking about acting on the basis of what God has done! You cannot live the Christian life on the basis of humanistic psychology. While you might succeed in living a fairly decent life, it is not "the Christian life."

The Christian life is lived out on the basis and foundation of what God has done in Christ Jesus. God's complete solution to the human dilemma caused by the historical fall of Adam is found in, and only in, another set of historical facts; namely, the death, resurrection, and ascension of our Lord Jesus Christ. *This is a vital truth!* Since our corrupted human nature was determined by the historical fall of Adam, our new identity and life is determined by the historical redeeming work of Jesus Christ.

The events that occurred in the city of Jerusalem nearly 2000 years ago were decisive events which affected all of mankind, whether they know it or not. In those events are all the benefits and provisions of God whereby we are set free from ourselves and granted a new life in Christ. God's purpose in sending Jesus into this world was to reverse the results of the fall of Adam whereby all of mankind was corrupted through sin. For this reason, Jesus is referred to in Scripture as the "last Adam" (1 Corinthians 15:45). The apostle Paul writes in Romans 5:18:

> Consequently, just as the result of one trespass was condemnation for all men, so also the result of one act of righteousness was *justification that brings life* for all men [emphasis mine].

In order to solve the human dilemma, God included and identified all mankind—all of Adam's children—in his only-begotten Son, our Lord Jesus Christ. As our human life is the result of our identification with Adam since we were born "in Adam," so God grants to us a new beginning, a new identity, and a new life by identifying us with Christ Jesus. We are born again "in Christ." This biblical truth involves a great many practical results in terms of our identity and life. It is a very neglected truth which has, for the most part, not been clearly taught in the church. In 1 Corinthians 1:30 Paul writes: "It is because of him (God the Father) that you are *in Christ Jesus!*" [emphasis mine].

The Cross of Jesus Christ

Because God has included us in Christ Jesus, whatever happened to Jesus also objectively, in the eyes of God, happened to us. If my house burns to the ground, whatever is contained in my house is also destroyed. If God included us in Christ Jesus, his history becomes our history.

The answer to the question, "Why should I separate from myself and reject myself?" is found in the truth that in the eyes of God, we died with Christ. The judgment measured against Christ is the judgment measured against the whole world of sinners. His death was the death of all men and is the *God-imposed act of judgment upon the children of Adam,* even though the sentence was executed upon the Son of God. The execution of Jesus on the cross is a *vicarious* act. Jesus died in our place, for us, instead of us. Because he had to die, God has judged us as being dead. We died with Christ.

We will not understand the meaning of, nor grasp in faith the new life offered in Christ *until we are willing to pass the same judgment upon ourselves that God has already passed upon us through the cross*. The death of Jesus Christ passed a total, complete judgment upon everything that we are, everything we have done regardless of whether it is good or bad, and everything that we possess in terms of natural gifts, skills, abilities, etc.[6] Because Jesus died, *we are dead!* We have been canceled out by the cross. God looked at fallen humanity, born out of the perverted root of Adam, and declared, "You are the problem and must be executed!"

The cross of Jesus Christ grants to us the only accurate estimate of ourselves and the only relief from ourselves. The implications of the cross are not pretty. Because Jesus died for us and we were included in him, *we are to consider ourselves as being dead.* Paul writes in 2 Corinthians 5:14 (KJV), "If one died for all, then were all dead!" In Galatians 2:20 we read, "I have been crucified with Christ!" We are to think of ourselves as being dead to sin (Romans 6:11), dead to the law (Romans 7:4), and dead to the world (Galatians 6:14). The apostle does not merely speak of this reality as a doctrinal or theoretical point. In Romans 6, for example, he asks the very practical question, "Should we continue to live in sin in order that grace might abound?" He answers the question by saying, "How can we who died to sin continue to live in it?"

Application

The outworking and application of this truth is in the manner in which we regard and judge ourselves. The Holy Spirit calls us to separate from ourselves as separating from that which is dead. Regarding yourself as dead is the ultimate act of self-rejection. It is one thing to feel bad about yourself; it is something far more intense to consider yourself a "dead thing." "Feeling bad about yourself" is considered to be a "psychological sickness" which, according to God's judgment, should be regarded as a "sickness unto death."

Because the death of Jesus was our death, living with ourselves and unto ourselves means living with a "dead thing." Jesus calls us to separate from the "dead thing," to lose our lives, to deny ourselves and cling in faith to him. Paul wrote: "We are convinced that one died for all, and therefore all died. And he died for all, that those who live should no longer live for themselves but for him who died for them and was raised again" (2 Corinthians 5:14,15).

A person who dies is free—free from any good works and free from any evil works. The person is free from worry and fear, free from sin and death. Centering and focusing attention upon self is merely digging up the corpse, so to speak. If you know that you have died with Christ, how can you feel good about yourself? A funeral director may make up and neatly dress a corpse, and the family may gather around the open casket and say, "Doesn't he look good?" but the cold facts are, the corpse is dead no matter how good it may look.

The Dealings of God

While the fact that we died with Christ is an objective reality since it is true outside of our experience, it is the work of the Holy Spirit to work this death within us subjectively through the various difficulties, disappointments, problems, temptations, and hardships of life. Through these dealings of God, we are motivated to become disappointed and "fed up" with ourselves and our "dead works" so that we might "get off self" and live our new life in Christ Jesus. In order to accomplish this work, God may even employ the assaults of the devil. Paul spoke of himself as being plagued by a "messenger of Satan" which God refused to remove lest Paul would become too highly exalted (2 Corinthians 12:8-10). In 2 Corinthians 4:10,11, Paul describes the death within him by saying:

> We always carry around in our body the death of Jesus so that the life of Jesus may also be revealed in our body. For we who are alive are always being given over to death for Jesus' sake, so that his life may be revealed in our mortal body.

A few years ago a leading televangelist who had fallen into sin came before his television audience and, with tears streaming down his face, declared, "I don't understand what happened to me." This was a very sad situation, but not because the man fell into sin. It was sad because he did not understand what happened to him. What happened was obvious. His pride, ambition, and relentless judgment and condemnation of other Christians was a greater threat to the kingdom than his immoral behavior. God allowed this man's weakness to be manifested in order to deliver him to the death of the cross and thereby set him free from sin. Concerning Martin Luther's understanding of suffering and testing, Paul Althaus wrote: "God leads us precisely into those situations that will stimulate and tempt our old man to sin. He does this in order to set us free from sin."[7] While it is true that today this man's ministry is not as powerful as it used to be, it seems that his attitudes and demeanor have been positively adjusted. He is certainly far more gracious and understanding toward the weaknesses of other Christians.

Most Christians today do not realize how important weakness, failure, discouragement, disappointment, suffering, testing, and trials are in the development of their Christian life. Through these dealings of God our natural sinful pride is being dealt with. God calls us away from ourselves so that through burying, rejecting, and denying self we may turn in faith unto our Lord Jesus and experience his life, peace, joy, and power. The apostle Paul wrote, "I will boast all the more gladly about my weaknesses, so that Christ's power may rest on me" (2 Corinthians 12:9).

The Real Enemy

Even though the Bible clearly teaches that every branch that bears fruit gets pruned (John 15:2) and "the Lord disciplines those he loves" (Hebrews 12:6), many Bible teachers today promote the heresy that Jesus has taken upon himself all the dealings of the Father so that we might experience his positive blessings, be enlarged, and be comfortable and prosperous in this world. They fail to recognize that we are the problem and God's purpose is to daily deliver us to the work of the cross so that we might leave self behind. Those who offer this teaching to the church are thereby confirming the children of God in childish immaturity.

Because of this error, many Christians have failed to learn the value of the disciplining work of God and never come to the place of turning away from self. Rather, contrary to his will, they seek God to enlarge and prosper self. For this reason, they never mature in their relationship with God nor discover all their sufficiency in Christ Jesus. They are unable to understand how it is that they can experience various sufferings and even be allowed to fall into sin. Even though they go through their ritualistic binding of the devil and confess the positive promises of the Word of God, nothing works. This seductive "faith teaching" is embraced by many Christians. It is far more popular to blame the devil than to see yourself as the cause of your own problems. To claim "the devil made me do it" is a cop-out.

In dealing with Christians, the devil does not operate through direct confrontation. While he is shrewdly working behind the scenes, the manifest enemy is not the devil, but our own sinful, self-centered, and proud human existence. In the Garden of Eden, it was not the purpose of the devil to tempt Eve to make a choice between worshiping him and worshiping God. Eve would have never given in to that temptation. The choice was between human pride—the desire to be like God—and worshiping and serving God himself. After Adam and Eve fall into sin, the devil drops out of the picture. You hear very little about him in the Old Testament. Once man is corrupted and turns in on himself, he will disobey God and destroy his fellowman without the devil reminding him to do so.

When Jesus determined to do the will of his Father in heaven and thereby deny his own life, the devil appeared on the scene. The three temptations that he used in the wilderness against Jesus were not directed at committing any great sins against God but were temptations directing Jesus to live unto himself, to be concerned with his own comforts, and to preserve his own life.

Many people are concerned today by the increase in occult activities and the growing popularity of Satan worship. While these activities are certainly dangerous and destructive, they also serve as a smoke screen blinding us to the real enemy in the church which is the self-esteem, positive confession, and positive-self-image teaching. These teachings seduce the people of God into focusing their attention upon enlarging themselves, feeling good about themselves, and even in some situations, desiring to be like God. Many people today have fallen into this snare of the devil.

The devil doesn't care how religious we are as long as we live for ourselves, remain consciously wrapped up in ourselves, try to feel good about ourselves, and cover up the nakedness of empty, meaningless lives through a spiritual charade. Martin Luther wrote concerning self-indulgence and human pride: "Against this secret villain we must pray God daily to suppress our self-esteem."[8]

How Badly Do You Hurt?

There are many hurting, unhappy, discouraged people in our world today. They struggle with their little problems and failures, chasing after every flimsy hope that is held out to them whereby they might overcome and find relief from their personal fears, broken hearts, worries, guilt, and feelings of inadequacy. They buy self-help books, undergo counseling, and seek to discover some gimmick, some way of thinking or acting that will provide relief.

If you are one of these hurting people, the question is: Are you hurting enough to give up on yourself? Are you unhappy enough and miserable enough to turn away from yourself with all your problems and failures and seek relief in a relationship with the person of Jesus Christ? Many claim to be hurting but are really not hurting enough. They are like the young woman I spoke of earlier who adamantly responded to my offering of a relationship with Jesus Christ, "I am not ready for that yet!" Jesus is the answer and does provide help, relief, comfort, peace, and joy, but surrendering and giving up on self is a prerequisite.

I believe it was Watchman Nee who told the story about the time that he was standing on a dock by the side of a lake. Next to him was a friend who happened to be an excellent swimmer. They were both watching a man who was swimming a rather long way from the shore. All of a sudden the man in the water got into trouble. He began to scream for help and thrash the water. Nee turned to his friend and excitedly asked,

"Aren't you going to help him? The man is in trouble."

"Not yet," his friend calmly answered.

A few moments passed and the man in the lake went down and came up again, struggling and fighting for air.

"Save him! Save him!" Nee begged.

"Not yet," his friend calmly responded.

Finally, the man stopped thrashing the water and all was calm. Nee's friend jumped into the water and with expert strokes swam to the drowning man and began to pull him to shore. Arriving at the shore, Nee's friend administered aid, and the drowning man, coughing and sputtering, was revived.

After the incident was over, Nee confronted his friend. "Why did you wait so long to save this man? He could have drowned!"

"I had no other choice," his friend responded. "If I would have gone to him immediately, he would have panicked and pulled me down with him. I had to wait until he stopped kicking. Then I could save him."

Are you willing to stop kicking? Are you willing to see all your little problems and unresolved conflicts, discouragements and disappointments, bad habits, negative attitudes, faults, and failures as being means whereby God is at work bringing you to the end of yourself? Are you willing to be nailed to the cross of Christ and buried in the waters of your baptism?

Get off yourself! You are the problem. Reject yourself! Forget about yourself. You are beyond help. God has given to you Jesus who is your help. C.S. Lewis writes at the very end of *Mere Christianity:*

> Look for yourself, and you will find in the long run only hatred, loneliness, despair, rage, ruin, and decay. But look for Christ and you will find him, and with him everything else thrown in.[9]

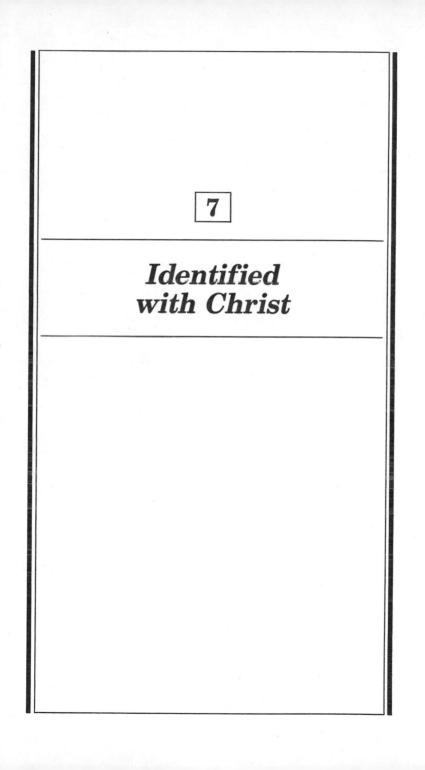

7

Identified with Christ

*"Your life is now hidden with
Christ in God"*
—St. Paul

When we turn away from and reject self and turn unto
Jesus, the very first thing that he gives to us is a new,
lofty personal identity in him. No longer must we "find
ourselves" in the various means of identification offered
by this world. No longer do we need other people to
bolster our flagging sense of self-worth. Our endless
quest to be somebody and to gain power, influence, fame,
and fortune comes to an end. The identity that God gives
to us in Christ Jesus lifts us far higher than anything
this world can offer. What is this new, personal identity?

As I shared with you, God included and identified all
mankind, all of Adam's children, in his Son, Jesus
Christ. His death was the death of all men. Through the
resurrection of our Lord Jesus, God *brought into being a
new creation.* Paul wrote, "Therefore, if anyone is *in
Christ,* he is a new creation; the old has gone, the new
has come" (2 Corinthians 5:17).

In Christ Jesus, God has declared the entire world of sinners forgiven. He has credited to their account the perfect righteousness of Jesus Christ and reconciled "the world unto himself." I am not promoting Universalism. The divine declaration of justification must be received and appropriated by faith. This is why we preach the gospel—so that the Holy Spirit will create the faith which grasps God's provision in Christ Jesus.[1] The apostle Paul writes in the fifth chapter of Romans:

> For just as through the disobedience of the one man the many were made sinners, so also through the obedience of the one man the many will be made righteous (v. 19).

As the result of the obedience of Jesus Christ, God has given us a new designation. In Adam we are called "sinners." In Christ we are called "righteous." We died with Christ, and we have been raised with Christ to a new life.

In the Ascension

When you search the pages of the New Testament in seeking to answer the question "What is our God-given personal identity?" you discover that God has not given us an identity on this earth. We are strangers, foreigners, and pilgrims. Our real personal identity is in the heavenly places since God has also identified us with the ascension of our Lord Jesus Christ.

The truth that God has identified us with the ascension of Jesus Christ is a very exciting truth which can literally lift our hearts out of the conflicts of this present life and into the heavenly places. It is not surprising that people have so much difficulty trying to find themselves in this world. They are looking in the wrong place. They are not looking up. In Ephesians 2:4-6 the apostle writes:

But because of his great love for us, God, who is rich in mercy, made us alive with Christ even when we were dead in transgressions—it is by grace you have been saved. And God raised us up with Christ and seated us with him in the heavenly realms in Christ Jesus.

A number of years ago, as I was wrestling with the teachings of Paul, I was unable to see or grasp what he meant when he wrote that we were seated in the heavenly places. The words of Paul which really stumped me were in Colossians 3:1-4. He wrote:

Since, then, you have been raised with Christ, set your hearts on things above, where Christ is seated at the right hand of God. Set your minds on things above, not on earthly things. *For you died, and your life is now hidden with Christ in God.* When Christ who is your life appears, then you also will appear with him in glory.

I could grasp the idea that I had died with Christ. This truth changed my way of thinking. I was dead to sin, dead to the world, dead to self.

I could even grasp the idea that I had been raised with Christ and was therefore a new creature. Because I was raised with Christ, I tried very hard to think of myself as being a "born-again, Spirit-filled, victorious saint in this world," but this caused me all kinds conflicts and guilt because my life did not agree with my resurrected identity. While I wanted to believe and would confess that I was a new, victorious creature because I was resurrected with Christ, I could not get my behavior, my attitudes, and my life to go along with my confession.

The conflicts were caused by the fact that I was unable to understand the significance of the fact that God had also identified me with the ascension of Jesus Christ.

One day, while walking the streets of beautiful downtown Omaha, Nebraska where I was speaking at a church that evening, I was meditating upon those verses from Colossians 3. I was prayerfully asking the questions "What did the apostle Paul mean when he said that I was dead and my real life was hidden with Christ in God? What does it mean that Christ is my life? Open my eyes, Lord!"

After a few moments, the thought hit me: "If in God's eyes you ascended into the heavenly places in Christ Jesus, then, as far as God is concerned, you are not even here. *You are where Jesus is!* For this reason, you have no identity here on this earth. You have no reason to even be concerned with yourself. From God's perspective, you have no life to improve and no righteousness or holiness to call your own. You have no great ministry in which you can boast. You are dead, and the person of Christ Jesus, dwelling within you by the Holy Spirit, is your only life."

This was a revolutionary, eye-opening thought which changed my entire approach to myself. At the time, it struck me as being very funny that I had been so wrapped up in myself when in the eyes of God, I was not even here. I began to laugh. I have often wondered what some of the people who passed me on the streets, giving me weird looks, were thinking.

"We Are Where He Is"

The truth is, God put us to death with Christ, made us alive in the resurrection, and raised us up with Christ in the ascension. Our personal identity is in the heavenlies. While the death of Jesus frees us from the "negative self," his ascension frees us from trying to find a "new spiritual self," which can be just as big a problem. It is no fun trying to act spiritual in the company of other people who are trying to act spiritual. They may see through your act. By identifying us with the ascension of

Jesus, God took us out of the picture completely. Having been identified with Christ, *we are where he is!* Our citizenship is in heaven. Our real life is hidden with Christ in God.

If God would have only identified us with the death and resurrection of our Lord Jesus Christ, we would still have every reason to become engrossed and centered in ourselves—our new spiritual, Christian, holy selves. Because of this failure to identify "self" with Christ Jesus in his ascension, many today boast of their new identity here on this earth. They strive to build their self-image upon what God has done for them. They talk about their spiritual gifts and their victorious Christian lives. They seek to build and defend their great ministries so that they might be known as "great men of God." Nothing has changed! They are still wrapped up and indulged in self.

Human Weakness/Divine Strength

The apostle Paul when looking at himself never enlarged himself, boasted of himself, or gave a testimony of his victorious Christian life. His identity in Christ Jesus was not in this world. His own "earthly identity" was found in Adam. This reality never changed. In fact, Paul felt foolish when put into the position of speaking of his own accomplishments (2 Corinthians 11). He was not concerned with himself. His negative self-image was not adjusted by his relationship with Jesus. In 2 Corinthians 12:9 he speaks about boasting of his weaknesses so that the power of Christ would rest upon him. When he looked upon his life that was lived upon this earth, he saw only his human weakness. Paul saw himself as weak, but Christ within him as strong. He downgraded himself, spoke of his weaknesses and his sufferings, called himself a wretch, and identified himself as the "chief of sinners."

But there are other times when Paul looked away from himself to the throne where he was seated with

Christ and found his identity in Christ. He was a conqueror! He was a saint! He was able to do all things through Christ! Whenever he took his focus away from the throne and gazed upon himself, he was weak and miserable. For this reason, he tells the Colossians: "Set your hearts on things above, where Christ is seated at the right hand of God."

This is a very important principle. When you look at yourself, you must see your sin. When you look away from yourself unto Christ Jesus, you see your new identity, your perfect righteousness, your glorious position with God in the heavenly places. Your life in this world, your peace, your joy and contentment is not dependent upon "how" you look. It depends upon "where" you look.

Right with God

Let us apply this principle of looking unto Jesus to the great doctrine of justification by faith. The doctrine of justification is the central teaching of the Christian church which fueled the Reformation of 1517. It speaks of our righteousness before God in Christ Jesus. It refers to our identity, the position which we have in Christ. There are many Christians who do not grasp the significance of justification because they do not understand the focus of justification. In seeking righteousness, they are looking in the wrong place.

In teaching a Bible class on the subject of justification by faith, I usually ask the question, "Do you have to be perfect to get to heaven?"

Often I will get the answer, "No! Nobody is perfect. If perfection was necessary, nobody would get to heaven."

But the truth is, you *do* have to be perfect in order to get to heaven and stand confidently in the presence of God. God is a perfectly righteous God and no imperfection can stand before him. The problem is, how are we going to become perfect? Where are we going to get perfect righteousness?

The good news of justification is that God has declared us perfect in Christ Jesus and has already seated us in the heavenly places. This is our identity. It is outside of us. By identifying us with Christ, God imputed to us the very righteousness of Christ. It was credited to our account. Christ is our righteousness.

We must be very careful to maintain that our righteousness before God is based upon what God has accomplished *in* Christ, not what we accomplish *for* Christ. We are righteous because God has identified us with Christ and has imputed to us the very righteousness of Christ. We can do good works and experience the peace and joy of the Lord because Christ is in us. Such a distinction is very important. To preserve our assurance of eternal life, we must maintain that our righteousness before God, wherein we shall stand before Him on the day of judgment, is not based on our good works, but because God has given to us a righteous identity in Christ Jesus.

Again, in teaching a Bible class I often ask another question: "How many of you are perfect?" Only those who understand justification by faith will raise their hand. The rest of the class may look at that "select group" as if to say, "Who in the world do you think you are?"

When I say "I am perfect!" I am not talking about my life. I am talking about an identity which God has given to me in Christ Jesus. When I look at Jesus, seated at the right hand of God, I see my perfect righteousness. When I look at myself, plodding along from day to day, getting old and facing inevitable death, I see my sin. The question is "Where do I choose to look?"

Those who are unable to confess, "I am perfectly righteous in Christ Jesus" have difficulty taking their eyes off themselves. In evaluating their own lives, they most certainly are not able to make that claim. But if they would look away from themselves and focus upon Jesus, they would find their identity. And what an identity it is! Just imagine—God has given to us perfection in Christ Jesus. He has identified us as being perfectly holy and righteous. Those who choose to manufacture their own self-image based on the opinions of other people would have great difficulty exceeding God's identification of us in Christ Jesus.

Therefore, *keep your eyes on Jesus*!

"I Shall Return"

Of course, the time will come when Jesus returns and we will be somebody in and of ourselves. Paul writes, "When Christ who is your life appears, then you also will appear with him in glory" (Colossians 3:4). When Jesus returns, we will have our own personal identity which will include our own righteousness and life. But for now, while we are on this earth, we have to live off the personal identity of someone else: Christ Jesus. Our lives are now hidden with Christ in God in the heavenly places.

Listen to what the apostle writes in 1 Corinthians 15:47-49:

> The first man was of the dust of the earth, the second man from heaven. As was the earthly man, so are those who are of the earth; and as is the man from heaven, so also are those who are of heaven. And just as we have borne the likeness of the earthly man, so shall we bear the likeness of the man from heaven.

While on this earth, we still bear the image of the earthly man, Adam, but we seek to live and walk in the life of the heavenly man, Christ Jesus. Because of the desire of the Holy Spirit within us to bring us into the fullness of what God has prepared for us, Paul writes, "We groan, longing to be clothed with our heavenly dwelling" (2 Corinthians 5:2). Our groaning is not because we lack joy and peace in our lives, but because such joy and peace is merely a foretaste, a down payment of what awaits us in heaven.

God has prepared for us an identity that will be ours for all eternity. But we have no identity on this earth. In and of ourselves, we are nobody. We are mere strangers and pilgrims. Our citizenship is in heaven. While we live on this earth, we must therefore live off the life of Christ Jesus. The apostle writes, "For to me, to live is Christ!" (Philippians 1:21). In Galatians 2:20 (KJV) he says, "I live; yet not I, but Christ liveth in me, and the life which I now live in the flesh I live by the faith of the Son of God."

I met a man some years ago who had been a government dignitary in Iran before the revolution. He had fled the country and was working as an attendant in a parking garage in New York City. He considered his job to be temporary. He was hoping one day to get back to his country and assume his rightful identity. He was a very sad person. It was not difficult to tell in talking to him that he was somebody at one time. In New York City, he was nobody because he had no connections. His real identity had been in Iran. Of course, if he had connections in high places in New York City, he would not have been working in a parking garage.

"He Is Where We Are"

While our identity is in the heavenlies because we are seated with Christ in the glory of the Father and we desire to take our rightful place in the eternal kingdom, we still have "connections" here on this earth. Because we have been identified with Christ, *he is where we are!* Many years ago, our Lord Jesus came down from the heavenlies and walked among men. He was in the same position that we are. When he returned to his Father, he said to his followers, "I am with you always." He sent his

Spirit into this world as a guarantee of what awaits us. While our personal identity is in heaven, as we live upon this earth Christ Jesus is our only life.

"Who Am I?"

The Christian life begins with a recognition of who we are in Christ. Speak the following confession out loud so that you can hear yourself declaring what God has said is true. You are not declaring these things to make them happen. God says that they have already happened! This is God's answer to the human question "Who am I?" This is who you are in Christ. Speak it with confidence.

THE CHRISTIAN'S PERSONAL IDENTITY

I believe that in Christ Jesus my sins have been fully and freely forgiven, and I am a new creation. I have died with Christ to my old identity in Adam. I have been raised with Christ to a new life. I am seated in the heavenly places in Christ Jesus. God has given to me the full righteousness of Jesus Christ. I am joined with angels, archangels, and all the saints in heaven. God is my Father, and if He is for me, who can be against me? Because of who I am in Christ, I am more than a conqueror. In fact, I can do all things through Christ Jesus who strengthens me. Christ Jesus is my life! Everything in my life here on this earth is working out for good according to the purposes of God. Christ Jesus Himself dwells within me. I have been called according to the purposes of God. These things I believe and confess, because God, my Father in heaven, says they are true. *Amen*!

This identity that you just confessed is true regardless of your day-to-day living. This is the meaning of grace. We are not worthy to be spoken of in this fashion. God does not look at us and declare that these things are true—He is looking at Jesus. As we look at Jesus, we see what God sees. We identify ourselves as God identifies us. If you should fall, your identity has not changed, no matter what the devil might try to tell you. Rise up! Brush yourself off. Receive your forgiveness. Lift up your eyes to the throne, and go on your way rejoicing.

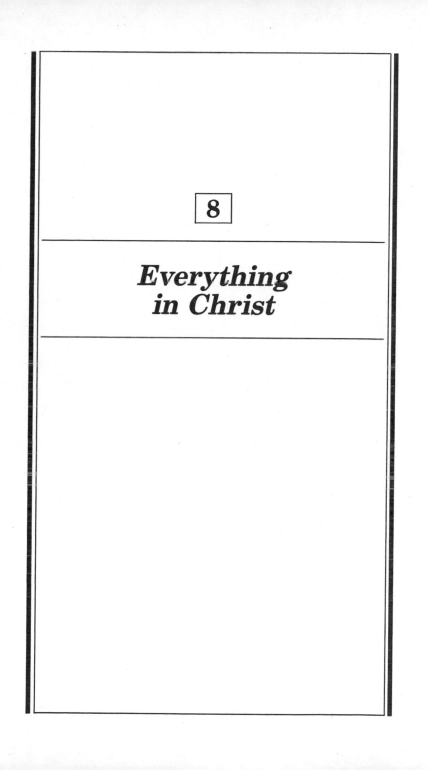

8

Everything
in Christ

*"It does not matter what
your personal deficiency . . .
God has always one sufficient answer,
His Son Jesus Christ, and He is the
answer to every human need."*
—Watchman Nee

I have often heard it said, especially among Christians who have had some glorious spiritual experiences, "Who needs doctrine? If we have the Holy Spirit, sound doctrine is not important." This is a very dangerous and damaging position.

I realize full well that many of the denominational churches of the past have been so very engrossed in getting their doctrinal definitions right that they have failed to speak to the basic spiritual needs of people. This has caused many "spiritual" Christians to think of doctrine as being totally divorced from life. As far as they are concerned, it has no practical value other than creating denominational barriers.

We must realize that doctrinal definitions determine the nature and quality of the life that exists within the Christian church. For example, think of how deeply the Roman Catholic doctrine of the Lord's Supper has distorted the spiritual life of Catholic people. By claiming that the bread and wine in the sacrament actually changes into the physical body and blood of Jesus, the people have been led to worship and adore a piece of bread. This is a doctrinal distortion. Think of the "Holiness Churches" and their doctrine of "perfect sanctification." The guilt, condemnation, and judgment of other Christians that exists among these people is the result of a false doctrine of the process of holiness.

There are many examples today of wrong doctrine and theology negatively influencing the lives of people. The "name, claim, prosperity teaching," which has led many into false expectations, is based upon a wrong theological definition of faith. The "Full Gospel" teaching, which includes physical healing within the redeeming work of Jesus Christ, leads those who remain in sickness to question their forgiveness and eternal life. In fact, one might even demonstrate that the moral failures of the big-name evangelists over the past few years is the result of a theological distortion of sanctification. Doctrinal definitions are not divorced from life but actually determine the nature and expression of the Christian life.

So put on your "thinking cap," and let us discuss the very important biblical definitions and doctrines regarding our new identity and life in Christ Jesus.

Identity and Life

The two themes of identity and life are central in the inspired teachings of the apostle Paul. He tells us that *in Christ* we discover our identity. This is an objective truth and defines our position with God. We are righteous. We have been justified. The Christian life, on the other hand, is lived *through Christ* who dwells within us by the Holy Spirit. This produces subjective Christian experience and is defined as sanctification. Making this distinction in reading and understanding the epistles of

Paul is very important. On some occasions, he is speaking about our identity—who we are in Christ Jesus. On other occasions, he is referring to our daily living—what results are produced through the new life of Christ dwelling within us.

Think of what happens if we confuse identity and life. If I try to apply my perfectly righteous identity in Christ to my human life, I will be filled with guilt and condemnation. If, on the other hand, my sinful human life becomes my identity before God, I will experience doubt over whether or not my sins are actually forgiven and that I am going to heaven. So, we must distinguish our identity in Christ from our life lived upon this earth.

As we discover our identity by looking unto Jesus in faith, so also we live the Christian life by looking unto Jesus. Our identity is defined as *justification*. The life we live by looking unto Jesus is defined as *sanctification*. While these two important doctrines cannot be divided or separated, they must be distinguished.

It is of great importance for us to realize that God has given to us one gift: *His Son.* In that one gift, God has given to us everything. There is a profound simplicity in Christianity. Everything begins and ends with the person of Jesus Christ. God does nothing in us directly—he has done everything in Christ Jesus! We have been included in Christ. This grants us a new identity. Through the hearing of the gospel, the Holy Spirit brought us to faith in Jesus. He now dwells in us. This grants to us a new life. Because I *am in Christ,* I have a new identity in the heavenly places. Because *Christ is in me,* I can live a new life. Jesus is the Alpha and Omega, the beginning and the end. In answer to all your questions, God has given Jesus to you! It is that simple.

The Inner Christ

Experiencing the joy, peace, hope, and contentment that are a part of the Christian life is the spontaneous result of the life of Christ dwelling within us through the Holy Spirit. While our identity is in the heavenlies, the indwelling Christ is our life. Jesus promised in John 15 that if we abide in him (find our identity with him in the heavenlies) and he abides in us (where we stay connected to his life within us), together we will bring forth much fruit. In Colossians 1:27 the apostle Paul speaks of the glorious mystery that has been revealed to the saints, which is "Christ in you, the hope of glory." Seeking to live the Christian life means that we *find ourselves in Christ and seek an ongoing, life-affecting experience with the Christ who dwells in us.*

The fact that Christ dwells in us is not the source of our identity, nor is "the inner Christ" to be the object of our focus. A person might mistakenly declare, "Sure I am a sinner, but Christ dwells in me. Therefore, I must be okay." Being right with God is based upon what God has done outside of us, in Christ. It is not based on the fact that Christ has chosen to dwell within us. The stance of the Christian is always extroverted. We are always looking away from ourselves, unto the throne, where we are seated in the heavenly places.

Mysticism

In various segments of the Christian church today, there is a dangerous, growing emphasis upon the alleged mystical encounter with the inner Christ. Mysticism seeks to discover the "Christ-self" within the depth of the human psyche or, as some suggest, within the unconscious mind. The revival of mysticism today is largely attributable to the influence of the popular philosophy of psychiatrist Dr. Carl Jung.

A "Christian" mystic alters his state of consciousness by eliminating all thoughts from his mind and entertaining the images in his imagination. By producing a meditative state, the mystic believes that he is actually visualizing Christ and entering into a dialogue with

him. Some mystics also engage in the practice of "jour-
naling" the "words of Jesus" received in their mystical
encounter.

I realize that there are many committed Christians
who love the Lord Jesus and, out of a desire to draw
closer to him, have embraced the practice of mysticism.
The practice is deceptive and dangerous. It demands an
introverted focus which is not taught in Scripture.
While I accept a "mysticism of the Word" and believe
that we actually encounter Christ in the gospel as the
Holy Spirit supernaturally enlightens our understanding, I cannot embrace a mysticism which directs my
focus unto myself, in order to look within myself.

It is very necessary to hold fast to the truth that *faith
always looks unto the Christ who is outside of us, not the
Christ within.*[1] This is a very important principle! The
stance of the Christian toward himself must always be
one of self-accusation. We are always related to the
earthly man. We never escape from the cross, which
continually delivers us to death. While the law directs us
into ourselves to discover our sin, the gospel always calls
us out of and away from ourselves so that, rejecting
ourselves as rejecting a "dead thing," we turn unto the
person of Christ Jesus. Anytime we become introspec-
tive, we should discover sin and death. When we look
away from ourselves unto Jesus, we discover righteousness and life. Mysticism is a very dangerous practice
because it distorts the focus of the Christian.

Not Spirituality

Usually in any work dealing with the Christian life
the subject of the spiritual side of the human personality
is a part of the discussion. I have purposely avoided that
subject. I do not believe that we are capable of discern-
ing, in and of itself, the pure distinction between what is
spiritual and what is not spiritual. Such a distinction
only becomes real when it is related to and determined

by our concrete, objective, active pursuit of the person of Jesus Christ. The person of Jesus Christ *is our spirituality*. Rather than speaking of "becoming more spiritual," we should rather think in terms of growing in our daily faith relationship with our Lord Jesus. This is as spiritual as we can get.

At the time of the Reformation of 1517, Martin Luther properly avoided speaking of Christian growth in terms of a deepened or "intensified spirituality." German theologian Werner Elert explains:

> Nor does Luther's faith want to be an intensified "spirituality." In the claim to have this intensified "spirituality," he sees a recollection of the temptation "You will be like God" and at all events the beginning of the end of faith.[2]

When we consider the "spirituality" of this age, Luther's position is certainly relevant, even if it was said in the sixteenth century. As it was true in Luther's time, we also are living in a very "spiritual" age. The New Age movement and the new mystical "transpersonal" psychology offers to people various spiritual pursuits such as meditation, visualization, contact with "spirit guides," out-of-body experiences, and the like. There have been attempts to define spirituality in physical terms by claiming that the right side of the brain is the seat of spirituality. Others have used Sigmund Freud's obscure psychological concept of the "unconscious mind" to locate the seat of human spirituality.[3] There are many spiritual people in our world who are not Christians.

The time has come for Christians to stop talking about spirituality and concentrate more on talking about Jesus. I do not like to be identified or to identify others as being "deeply spiritual." Such a definition can mean many things. I would prefer to speak of a person as having a relationship with Jesus Christ. While you can have spirituality apart from Jesus, you cannot have Jesus without the Holy Spirit. Relating to the person of Jesus Christ from day to day is the extent of our spirituality.

Not Spiritual Things, But Jesus

Contrary to the thinking of many Christians, God does not grant to us a host of spiritual benefits and experiences. Our human pride would like to have spiritual benefits and experiences in order to enlarge ourselves and be identified as "deeply spiritual people." God does not offer to us forgiveness, righteousness, love, peace, joy, gifts, ministries, wealth, and prosperity as separate entities. Since our identity is in the heavenly places, we cannot claim anything that comes from God as belonging unto us. God has only given to us one thing: *His Son Jesus Christ,* who is our life. In Christ are all of the blessings and benefits of life and salvation. The Bible says:

> Praise be to the God and Father of our Lord Jesus Christ, who has blessed us in the heavenly realms with every spiritual blessing in Christ (Ephesians 1:3).
>
> It is because of him that you are in Christ Jesus, who has become for us wisdom from God—that is, our righteousness, holiness and redemption (1 Corinthians 1:30).
>
> That they may know the mystery of God, namely, Christ, in whom are hidden all the treasures of wisdom and knowledge.... So then, just as you received Christ Jesus as Lord, continue to live in him, rooted and built up in him... and you have been given fullness in Christ (Colossians 2:2,3,6,7,10).

> His divine power has given us everything we
> need for life and godliness through our knowl-
> edge of him who called us by his own glory and
> goodness (2 Peter 1:3).

One of the books that has influenced my understanding of the Christian faith and life is the classic work of
Chinese evangelist Watchman Nee titled *The Normal
Christian Life.* His understanding of the singular all-
sufficiency of Christ is profound. Nee writes:

> God will not give me humility or patience or
> holiness or love as separate gifts of his grace.
> He is not a retailer dispensing grace to us in
> packets, measuring out some patience to the
> impatient, some love to the unloving, some
> meekness to the proud, in quantities that we
> take and work on as a kind of capital. He has
> given only one gift to meet our need: His Son
> Christ Jesus. As I look to Him to live out His
> life in me, He will be humble and patient and
> loving and everything else I need—in my
> stead....It does not matter what your per-
> sonal deficiency, or whether it be a hundred
> and one different things, God has always one
> sufficient answer, His Son Jesus Christ, and
> He is the answer to every human need.[4]

It is very important for our understanding and experience of the Christian life that we recognize that all
Christian benefits, gifts, and fruit are found in the person of Christ Jesus who dwells within us. They belong to
Jesus, not to us. As a result of various movements and
emphases within the church, Christian consciousness
often becomes directed at various spiritual pursuits.
Some Christians go after inner, mystical experiences.
Others attempt to discover their spiritual gifts or want

to learn how to speak in tongues or to heal people. Many Christians today are pursuing prosperity or success as a characteristic by-product of being a Christian. Sanctification is desired as a reflection of individual personal holiness and morality. This separation of the content of the Christian life and experience from the person of Jesus Christ is no small matter! It will inevitably lead into numerous distortions such as humanism, mysticism, occultism, or legalism.

Our "religious" focus is not to be directed at spiritual gifts and blessings but at the person of Jesus Christ. If we desire the forgiveness of sins and a righteousness that is acceptable to God, *God gives us Jesus*. If we seek peace, joy, and love, *God gives us Jesus*. If we desire comfort in the midst of sorrow, hope when things look hopeless, assurance when plagued by doubt, and contentment through the changing scenes of life, *God gives us Jesus*. All spiritual gifts are simply manifestations of the new life of Christ dwelling with us, manifested spontaneously as we walk in the Spirit by directing our consciousness unto Jesus.

The theme of the letter of Paul to the Colossians is the centrality of Jesus Christ. The substance of the Christian faith, according to the apostle Paul, is found in the person and work of Christ. He warns the Colossians against seeking spiritual substance outside of Christ. He writes:

> See to it that no one takes you captive through hollow and deceptive philosophy, which depends on human tradition and the basic principles of this world *rather than on Christ* (2:8; emphasis mine).
>
> Therefore, do not let anyone judge you by what you eat or drink, or with regard to religious festival.... These are a shadow of the

things that were to come; *the reality, however, is found in Christ* (2:16; emphasis mine).

Do not let anyone who delights in false humility and the worship of angels disqualify you for the prize. Such a person goes into great detail about what he has seen, and his unspiritual mind puffs him up with idle notions. *He has lost connection with the Head* (2:18; emphasis mine).

When we receive Christ Jesus as our Lord and Savior, all of the benefits found in Christ Jesus become our possession. We have his peace and joy, his righteousness and holiness. His love is shed abroad in our hearts through the Holy Spirit. In fact, the Bible tells us that in Christ we are complete and fulfilled. The gospel of Jesus Christ is truly a message of good news that calls us away from and out of ourselves and unto Jesus! We discover everything "in Christ" and will find nothing "outside of Christ." "Christ is all and in all!"

In the gospel according to John, our Lord Jesus speaks of himself as being the very essence of all the blessings and promises of God. He is "the way and the truth and the life" (John 14:6). At Lazarus' tomb, Jesus did not speak of *resurrection* as being a reward for a life well-lived. He said, "I *am* the *resurrection*." After feeding the 5000, he offered himself as being the very bread that came down from heaven. He is the light of the word. He is the water of life. He is the good shepherd. "In Him was life, and that life was the light of men" (John 1:4).

"We Put on Christ"

In Galatians 3:27, the apostle Paul writes: "All of you who were baptized into Christ have clothed yourselves with Christ." When we came to faith in Jesus Christ and were baptized, we received all of the blessings that are in Christ. He became joined to us, so that whatever gifts, grace, peace, joy, or contentment are manifested in us, they belong to Christ. They belong to us because we have Christ dwelling within us.[5]

Because every Christian has Christ dwelling within through faith, it must therefore follow that every Christian possesses God's everything. While it is true that some Christians, as a result of personal deficiency and need, have seemingly appropriated more of the blessings that have been provided in Christ than have other Christians, they dare not declare or even remotely suggest, "I have something you don't have."

For example, a person who has passed through times of grief and turned in faith unto Jesus, discovered in him the source of deep, abiding comfort. He is thereby enabled to declare, "Christ is my comfort!" One who possibly has not shared the same need might not have discovered the same provision in Christ. This does not mean that such provision is not already his possession, ready to be grasped by faith. For if we have Christ and have put on Christ, we have everything.

We are seeking Jesus! There is nothing that we will find outside of Christ, nor will we discover anything worthwhile inside of us apart from Christ. We seek all things "in Christ"! This is a very important understanding. We don't say, "Christ has given me a new life" as if he has provided us with an identity here on this earth. Rather we say, "Christ is my new life." We don't say, "I am becoming holier and holier" as if our earthly identity is in a state of improvement. We do say, "Christ is manifesting his holiness in me." We don't say, "God has given to me certain spiritual gifts," as if we are becoming somebody in this world. We do say, "The ministry and power of Jesus is manifested in my earthly body." We don't talk about the "great men of God" on this earth, for there are none. No matter how high and lofty a position a person attains in the church of Jesus Christ or how much influence he is able to exert upon a large number of people, he remains a little, sinful man in whom is being manifested a great God and Savior, Jesus Christ!

What About Natural Gifts?

God created humankind with many natural gifts and abilities. They were a part of Adam's identity. Of course, when Adam fell into sin, these natural gifts and abilities were also corrupted. When God put us to death with Christ on the cross, our natural skills, abilities, and talents were also reckoned to be dead. Therefore, we cannot find our identity in our gifts and abilities. Our identity is always outside of us, in the heavenly places in Christ Jesus.

When we came to faith in Jesus Christ and were baptized, Christ entered into us and animated every part of our being. For example, think of yourself in this way. You are dead and laid out in a casket. Jesus comes and takes your hand. His life flows through you and quickens your being. Whereas before your natural skills and abilities belonged to you and were perhaps the source of your pride, now they belong to Christ. His life flows through them. Apart from Christ, they are merely associated with the "dead thing."

Before natural gifts and abilities are able to be used by the Lord Jesus they must be marked with the imprint of the cross. I knew a young man who was a very skilled guitar player. The ability was the source of his pride. At a young age he quit school and joined a touring "rock band." He became involved in the drug scene and was almost destroyed. As the result of the work of a youth ministry, he became a Christian and a committed part of a local church.

It took a number of years before he was able to use his guitar-playing ability within the worship life of his church. It was too closely related to his old identity in Adam. Only after he reckoned that skill to be a dead thing and not the source of his pride and identity, was he able to yield it to Jesus and use it in accompanying worship.

Natural skills and abilities are neutral. They can be animated by the "ol' Adam" or by the "alien" life of Christ dwelling within us. Adolph Hitler, for example, had a tremendous gift of public speaking. The gift was used to deceive an entire nation. It also could have been used to preach the gospel of Jesus Christ. The important thing is not the gift itself, but the life which animates the gift. "Ol' Adam" desires to use our gifts and abilites for our own pride and sense of self-worth. The Holy Spirit uses our gifts and abilities for the glory of God.

9

The Conflict

*"For the sinful nature desires
what is contrary to the Spirit, and the Spirit
what is contrary to the sinful nature."*
—St. Paul

It had been a beautiful Sunday morning experience.
The worship, the singing, and the choir had been magnificent. I had preached on my favorite subject of justification, and it seemed that the words just poured out of
me. As I walked home from church at noon, I felt like I
was walking on air. The joy and peace remained and
bubbled over as an afterglow of the worship experience.

I greeted my wife, Dianne, who was busily beginning
the Sunday dinner preparations.

"Wasn't that a great service?" I asked, fully expecting
a confirming response. Dianne was often very sensitive
to the quality of the worship service and the response of
the congregation. "Wow, the worship was fantastic.
Didn't the choir..."

"I didn't get anything out of it," she angrily interrupted.

"What do you mean you didn't get anything out of it? The worship was fantastic, and you didn't get anything out of it?" I responded incredulously. "How in the world anyone can sit in that church this morning and not get anything out of it..."

"Oh, it's easy for you," she again interrupted. "You are not stuck balancing a baby on your lap, juggling the hymnal, and trying to break up the arguments between the other two. I can't understand why those kids of ours can't behave themselves in church. They are always at each other. I get so mad sometimes I could scream."

My blood began to boil. I got up from the kitchen table and marched into the living room where the Sunday papers were spread out from one end to the other. The two older kids were laid out on the floor reading the comic sections.

"What's the matter with you two?" I angrily asked. "Why can't you behave in church? You got your mother all upset."

"He keeps teasing me," my older daughter explained, pointing the finger at my oldest son, who usually got the blame for most of the family squabbles—and often rightly so.

"Get out of here, both of you! I am sick and tired of looking at you! Go to your rooms!" I grabbed them both by an arm and marched them into their rooms and slammed the doors. I went back in the living room and angrily began gathering the papers together.

Amazingly, within about five minutes, the joy, peace, and sense of excitement which had been flowing within me as a result of a worship experience had been replaced with anger and frustration. What a difference five minutes can make.

This is not an abnormal situation. All Christians go through experiences of this nature. They may be "up" one moment, lifted up into the heavenly places, and "down" the next when they are again confronted with the reality of the old sinful nature. This is *normal Christian living*!

Because we have received all spiritual blessings in Christ Jesus does not mean that we live in and experience all of those blessings. Our life and experience here on this earth, even within Christian families, does not want to "line up" with our heavenly identity—and for good reasons. We live in the midst of a fallen world. Our old life received from Adam, though put to death with Christ, does not want to stay dead. Touched off by even the little negative circumstances of life, we quickly move from peace to frustration, from joy to anger, from praise and worship to arguments and personal conflicts.

A Double Life

The Bible speaks of us as containing two sources of life which are in conflict with each other. We were born into this world in Adam, and the old nature of Adam was joined to us. As a result of coming to faith in Jesus Christ through the hearing of the gospel, we were born again in Christ Jesus, and the life of Christ was joined to us. This is our condition.

As the result of our "double birth" in Adam and in Christ, while we are still upon this earth, we possess a double life. Paul refers to this double life as being "the old man" and "the new man," or the flesh (the sinful human nature) and the Spirit (Christ dwelling within). The life of Adam, which is our *human* life, will continue to adhere to us until we bury "the earthly man" in the dust from whence he came. The new life of Christ which also dwells within us is an *alien* life. It comes from a different world. It is the life of "the heavenly man." Commenting on this double life, Martin Luther writes in his *Commentary on Galatians:*

> There is a double life: my own which is natural or animate; and an alien life, that of

> Christ in me. So far as my animate life is concerned, I am dead and am now living an alien life.[1]

Because of this double life, the normal Christian experience is conflict. Attempting to change our natural earthly life and become more loving, kind, self-controlled, and considerate is a hopeless task. Our human life will not cooperate with our desire for self-improvement. Because of this, many Christians strive to live a charade and give the impression of deep spiritual maturity. Those of us in the public ministry often try to give the impression to our people that we have it together and are totally in control of our lower passions and desires. But, if you lived with any of the alleged "great Christians" and watched them in all situations of life, you would soon discover that they too live a double life. The fact of the matter is, every Christian who dresses up in his Sunday best and tries to impress others with his deep spirituality is a phony! In Galatians 5:17 the apostle writes:

> For the sinful nature desires what is contrary to the Spirit, and the Spirit what is contrary to the sinful nature. They are in conflict with each other, so that you do not do what you want.

If a Christian does not experience conflict, it is not because he has been conformed to his heavenly identity, but is more likely because he simply does what comes naturally, and lives according to the old sinful nature under the guise, "After all, I am only human." Many Christians simply give up on themselves and say, "This is the way I am." While their assessment of their human earthly condition is accurate, they do not take into consideration that they possess an alternative, alien life through Christ, "the heavenly man," dwelling within them.

Our desire should not be for self-improvement but to abide in this life of Christ Jesus dwelling within us. Paul speaks of this as "walking in the Spirit."

Walk in the Spirit

Living the Christian life simply means that we live according to our new life in Christ and not according to our old life in Adam. Understanding this reality is not difficult. It is like having a single water spout with both a cold and hot water faucet. What you turn on will be what you get! In Galatians 5:16 the apostle Paul instructs us to "turn on" our new life in Christ, or "the Spirit," and to "turn off" our old life in Adam, or "the flesh." Either faucet we turn on will produce different results.

The old sinful nature which adheres to us as a result of our birth in Adam is proud, rebellious, self-centered, worldly, and an enemy of God. It is continually demanding our conscious attention. Being dead, it produces dead works. By indulging our old sinful nature, we also reap the results of worry, fear, discontent, self-pity, anxiety, depression, and all of the other "blessings" of being human.

The new life of Christ which, as a result of our faith in Christ Jesus and our baptism whereby we "put on Christ," also adheres to us and is obedient, submissive, kind, loving, gentle, and a "friend of God." It produces life! The Holy Spirit is at work in us, urging us to live and walk in Christ Jesus. Paul writes, "Just as you received Christ Jesus as Lord, continue to live in him" (Colossians 2:6).

"Adam, Where Are You?"

While the concept of living the Christian life is quite simple, the difficulty arises when we attempt to identify in our daily experience what is of Adam and what is of

Christ. If we want to grow in our relationship with the Lord Jesus and "abide in him" as he has commanded, distinguishing our "old dead sinful nature" from the new life of Christ is very important. If we are unable to make such an identification, we will not know when to repent. How can we turn away from "ol' Adam" if we are not able to identify him? As is characteristic of Adam, he does not want to come out in the open. He hides himself.

When the Bible talks about "abiding in Christ" or "walking in the Spirit," it is not speaking about camouflaging "ol' Adam" behind a spiritual veneer. This is a common practice among so-called "spiritually renewed" people. One who by nature has a bad temper now speaks of himself as being filled with "righteous anger." One who may normally be very critical of others is now "practicing discernment." A person who manifests a "pushy" or overbearing personality is now "zealous for the Lord."

I have known many Christians who have become very spiritual people, but nothing really changed in their lives. "Ol' Adam" was merely given a spiritual paint job. I knew one man, for example, who was never able to hold down a job. After being "spiritually renewed," he claimed that it was the Lord who was always leading him into a variety of new occupations. He actually would stand up and witness in a prayer meeting to the new opportunities the "Lord" was opening up for him. Nothing had changed. I knew a woman who was by nature very opinionated. Rather than forcefully stating what she wanted, after she became "spiritual," she would wrap her opinions in "prophetic language" and declare, "Thus saith the Lord." One man I had known for years was very demanding of those around him. He always wanted to be the expert and tell other people how to think and how to live. When he became spiritual, his "gift of advice" was simply translated into a new dimension.

Now he was preaching at others about being good Christians. One independent church actually ordained him into the preaching ministry.

Identifying Ol' Adam

The Bible gives to us a way of clearly distinguishing our old sinful nature from our new life in Christ. We identify which is in control on the basis of results. In Galatians, the apostle Paul provides ample evidence by which we are enabled to determine who is in control of our lives. He writes:

> The acts of the sinful nature are obvious: sexual immorality, impurity and debauchery; idolatry and witchcraft; hatred, discord, jealousy, fits of rage, selfish ambition, dissensions, factions and envy; drunkenness, orgies, and the like (5:19-21).

But on the other hand:

> The fruit of the Spirit is love, joy, peace, patience, kindness, goodness, faithfulness, gentleness, self-control (5:22,23).

While we may be able to identify within ourselves and within others specific sins or actions that are contrary to the Ten Commandments, we fall short in identifying many of the actions and attitudes that proceed from our old sinful nature. "Ol' Adam" often hides himself behind what we might consider to be "human characteristics." While we may be willing to acknowledge and repent of obvious sins against God, we often ignore what we think of as the less-serious manifestations of our old sinful nature.

This failure to identify "ol' Adam" greatly hinders our Christian growth. We put up with various attitudes and actions that are a part of our daily experience because, after all, we are only human. It is these negative human characteristics which also destroy our peace, joy, love, and contentment. Because we are not happy, we may seek solutions in counseling and psychology rather than realizing that what we need is repentance. The solution to our negative human characteristics is not found in good advice but in separating from self and clinging to Jesus.

For example, for years I easily became caught up in self-pity. I did not regard it as a sin as such. Afterall, from time to time everybody feels sorry for themselves. It was a human characteristic. In order to feel better about myself, I embraced the thinking of modern psychology and sought to develop a positive self-image. When I came to the realization that self-pity is not merely a human characteristic but a manifestation of "ol' Adam" and a sin against God, I was more ready to repent and turn to Jesus. I can now confess that my identity in Christ and the life of Christ within me saves me from self-pity.

Consider some of the other popular manifestations of "ol' Adam."

Many Christians complain about their plight in life and gripe about the manner in which they are being treated by other people. Within the fellowship of the church of God there exists the continual undercurrent of complaining and bickering about what this one has done or what that one has said. Is this a sin against God? I am sure that many would say, "No. This is normal human behavior." But is this not a manifestation of our old sinful nature which needs to be acknowledged as sin? Definitely so.

How would you identify depression; loneliness; fear; anxiety; hurt feelings; critical spirit; negativism; discontent; confusion; gossip; impatience; being moody, unfriendly and inconsiderate; dishonesty; grumbling;

stubbornness; etc.? Are these sins? Violations of the Ten Commandments? While we may not speak of these attitudes as gross sins, they are most certainly clear manifestations of our old sinful nature.

The Alternative

While we are shocked when "gross sins" appear among the people of God, especially among those who are "spiritual" leaders, we are willing to overlook the clear manifestations of the old sinful nature that exist in our own lives and are rampant within the life of the church. Many of the attitudes of the old sinful nature that I have listed are present in every church meeting, whether it be youth meetings, ladies' guild, men's club, congregational meetings, or even church conventions which are dominated by the clergy.

Believers in Jesus Christ are not "locked in" to living in this fashion. God has granted to us a way of escape. Our new life in Christ provides an alternative. Do not be afraid to be unmerciful toward yourself in identifying "ol' Adam." Throw away the excuses and face reality! The fact that you are grumpy in the morning does not mean that "you got up on the wrong side of the bed." It means your old sinful nature is in control. Because you enjoy hearing some "dirt" about other people does not mean you have an inquisitive mind. It means that you are not abiding in Christ. Because you easily "blow your cool" does not mean you have a short fuse. It means you have a weak connection to Jesus.

Those who have no alternative life in Christ Jesus must preserve themselves and avoid accepting blame and responsibility. This is the only human response to the human condition. As believers in Jesus Christ, we are not "merely human." In addressing the conflicts and divisions that existed with the church at Corinth, Paul writes, "For since there is jealousy and quarreling among you, are you not worldly? Are you not acting like mere men?" (1 Corinthians 3:3).

The more willing we are to accuse ourselves and identify the manifestations of our old sinful nature, the
greater reason we will have for looking unto Jesus.
Don't worry about preserving human dignity. God has
granted to us a much better life in Christ Jesus.

Such an approach to life will certainly create far more
conflicts. We will no longer be willing to merely put up
with some of our "human characteristics." In the midst
of such conflicts, the Bible teaches us to consciously look
unto Jesus. Jesus is our victory over these human characteristics. His life in us produces love, joy, and peace.
We are called to turn away from ourselves and look unto
Jesus.

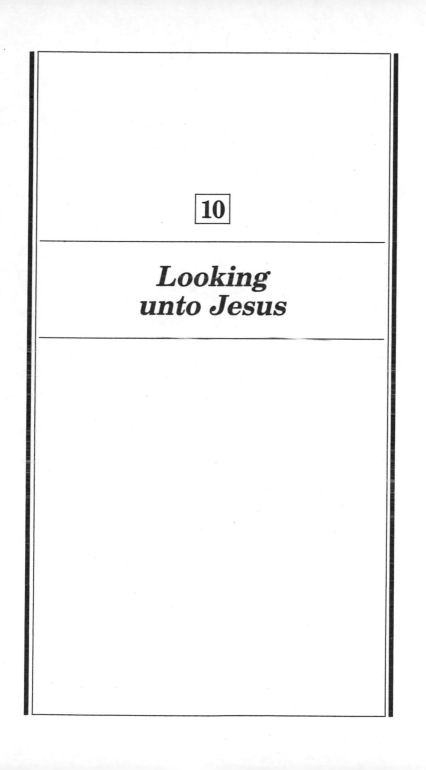

10

Looking unto Jesus

*"Thinking must be turned
in another direction, and Christ
must be thought of so that you may say,
Christ lives!"*
—Martin Luther

The Bible tells us to look unto Jesus and focus our lives upon him. Our faith does not behold the things that are seen, but rather the things that are unseen. By looking away from ourselves into the heavenlies where we are seated with Christ, we discover our new identity and also stir within ourselves the new life that God has granted to us in Christ. Jesus tells us to abide in him, and he will abide in us. The question is, how do you look unto Jesus? What are the principles involved?

The Bible is not merely a book of stuffy doctrines and the offer of "pie in the sky in the great by-and-by." The Word of God clearly explains to us the cause of our problems and sets before us a way of abiding in Christ. The biblical principles, especially those taught by the apostle Paul, are not laws in the sense of the Ten Commandments, but are principles governing *life*—the new life we share in Christ Jesus. The apostle taught the

Christians of the first century how to remain joined to the life that was in Christ Jesus on a day-to-day basis.

Have you ever wondered how the various churches in the first century were able to survive? Paul would journey into a city, preach the gospel, and the Holy Spirit would create faith in the hearts of people, bringing a church into being. Paul would then leave and travel to the next city. The church had no Bible, except the Old Testament. They had no pastors or trained counselors. Yet, they survived and grew. The letters that Paul wrote to many of these churches, especially Romans, Galatians, Ephesians, Philippians, and Colossians, reflected a level of spiritual maturity that most within the church today have not even touched or, for that matter, are even able to understand. It seems to me that the answer is found in the fact that Paul did not teach only doctrines and theology that were removed from life. He also taught the Christians how to stay joined to Jesus. It was the life of Christ within the individual Christians that produced the results. Listen to Paul's practical instructions....

Set Your Mind

After encouraging the Roman Christians to walk in the Spirit and not in the flesh, the apostle Paul provides some very practical and applicable instructions for living in Christ. In Romans 8:5,6 we read:

> Those who live according to the sinful nature have their minds set on what that nature desires; but those who live in accordance with the Spirit, have their minds set on what the Spirit desires. The mind of sinful man is death, but the mind controlled by the Spirit is life and peace.

Read those verses again, very carefully. Paul says that the mind set on the old sinful nature produces death. What does that mean? As we have already discussed, *we are dead.* We died with Christ. By setting the mind on our old sinful nature inherited from Adam, we are focusing upon the "dead thing." By our conscious attention, we are "digging up the corpse," so to speak. By setting our minds upon the desires of the Spirit, we are living in Christ. His life is stirred within us. His peace is our experience.

This theme of setting our conscious thinking upon the things of the Spirit is an important ingredient in the theology of Paul. In Philippians 4:8, we read:

> Finally, brothers, whatever is true, whatever is noble, whatever is right, whatever is pure, whatever is lovely, whatever is admirable—if anything is excellent or praiseworthy—think about such things.

Again we read in Colossians 3:1,2:

> Since, then, you have been raised with Christ, set your hearts [affections, the desires of the mind] on things above, where Christ is seated at the right hand of God. Set your mind on things above, not on earthly things.

In 2 Corinthians 10:4,5, the apostle speaks of our battle plan and the purpose of our spiritual warfare:

> The weapons we fight with are not the weapons of the world. On the contrary, they have divine power to demolish strongholds. We demolish arguments and every pretension that sets itself up against the knowledge of God, and we take captive every thought to make it obedient to Christ.

Consider some of the other directions of the apostle Paul. In Ephesians 4:22-24, he instructs us to put off the old man, *to be made new in the attitudes of our minds,* and to put on the new man. The same thought is shared in Romans 12:2. We are not to be conformed to the world, but transformed *by the renewing of our minds.* The very word "repentance" means to "change your mind." Throughout his epistles, Paul is continually urging us to rejoice in the Lord, to be filled with thanksgiving unto God, not to be anxious, fearful, or filled with worry. He tells us to sing psalms, hymns, and spiritual songs with gratitude in our hearts unto the Lord. All of these instructions are intended to direct our hearts and minds away from our old sinful nature and unto the new life that we have in Christ Jesus.

Beginning in the Mind

The works of the flesh listed in Galatians 5:19-21 are either characterized by or initiated by the attitudes of the heart and mind. The actions of the sinful nature begin as thoughts. Adultery and fornication, for example, begin with the mind occupied with lust. Stealing begins with coveting. Murder is identified with hatred. Our Lord Jesus in the Sermon on the Mount disturbed the religious Pharisees by equating the attitudes of the heart and mind with the sinful action itself. Even the foolish involvement in various elements of occultism or witchcraft is initiated via emptying the mind of all thoughts and entering into a mental trance. It is no wonder that the apostle Paul emphasized the need for Christians to establish their hearts and minds in Christ Jesus. The instructions of the apostle are very practical and are intended to produce an adjustment in our consciousness.

Since our minds are at the very center of our being, whether we live in old Adam or live according to our new life in Christ is related to the direction and substance of our thought-life. *This truth is the most important practical aspect of living and walking in the Spirit.* Learning this truth literally changed my life! In offering the solution to sadness and depression, Martin Luther advised: "Thinking must be turned in another direction, and Christ must be thought of so that you may say, Christ lives!"[1]

The problem is, we are not able to control the thoughts that come at us. Worry, fear, lust, anger, hatred, and self-pity will come knocking on our door, seeking to be entertained by us. The devil, the world, and our self-centered, sinful flesh are continually bombarding our minds with worries, fears, thoughts of sexual impurity, self-pity, resentment, bitterness, envy, and the like. It is one thing to have these thoughts enter your mind. It is something quite different to entertain them and dwell upon them. One of the old church fathers, in speaking about evil thoughts, said, "You cannot prevent the birds from flying in the air over your head, but you can certainly prevent them from building a nest in your hair."[2]

Positive Thinking

Possibly some will respond to this by saying, "What you are saying is no different than the 'positive thinking,' 'positive mental attitude,' 'possibility thinking' teachings that are so popular today." While it may appear on the surface that these techniques are of the same nature as the biblical teachings of the apostle Paul, there is a world of difference. It is very important for us to make a clear distinction.

Much "Christian" teaching today has become a mixture of theology, psychology, and New Age practices. The methods employed in modern psychology and the New Age movement are very similar to the practical instructions of the New Testament, with a singular, glaring exception: The New Testament focuses upon Jesus Christ.

Explaining the foundation of the approach of "positive thinking" and positive mental attitude, Dr. Gary Collins writes:

William James once concluded that the greatest discovery of his generation was the fact that "human beings can alter their lives by altering the attitudes of the mind." The quality of our lives is closely related to the quality of our thinking.[3]

This fact alone has become the basis of much counseling and self-help techniques. Dr. Collins writes:

The mind can control its own thinking and this in turn can influence behavior. This conclusion is the core of Norman Vincent Peale's popular philosophy of "positive thinking." It is the basis of Robert Schuller's theology of "possibility thinking." It is central to the "positive mental attitude" approaches to success. And it is the foundation assumption in a host of recent stress-management books and seminars.[4]

According to the positive thinker, the inherent power for adjusting the quality of human life is discovered within the parameters of the natural mind, in the technique of thinking itself. The positive thinker taps into that alleged inherent power in a number of ways. He can either focus his conscious mind upon health, wealth, prosperity, and a positive self-image, or positively program the alleged unconscious mind via subliminal motivation. "Christian" leaders such as Norman Vincent Peale and Paul Yonggi Cho teach the visualization of the desired result as a means for releasing the "power" within the mind. In this sense, the positive thinking/ possibility thinking movement is very much akin to mysticism.

While all of the positive-thinking techniques seem on the surface to be worthwhile and positively influence human behavior, the teaching is a major deception. The philosophy that undergirds the technique is not based upon truth. While the principles seem to be in line with Scripture, Jesus is eliminated.

Positive thinking and possibility thinking lead unsuspecting Christians away from looking to Jesus for their identity and life and push them back into focusing their minds upon themselves. While the Bible teaches us to judge the content of our natural life through self-accusation, positive thinking directs us to think highly of ourselves and to hold wonderful thoughts about ourselves. Many positive thinkers consider the consciousness of sin and guilt as negative thoughts which produce negative energy and should, under no circumstances, be confessed. Dr. Paul Vitz of New York University is correct in pointing out that possibility thinking is based upon faith in one's self and turns God into a mere servant who exists in order to help us achieve our goals.[5]

Fact, Not Fancy

In comparing the wishful thinking of positive thinking, possibility thinking, and positive mental attitude with legitimate Christianity, William Kilpatrick writes:

> That attitude, however, is the very antithesis of real Christianity, which insists that faith must be anchored in objective fact.... The Christian faith is not founded on beautiful thoughts but on decisive historical events.... It stands or falls on the reality of those events.[6]

All Christian practice is based upon the factual reality of the historical events of the death, resurrection, and ascension of our Lord Jesus. God included us in these events. God reveals these truths to us in his Word. Therefore, whatever stance we occupy and whatever practices we teach find their basis in those historical events.

Our new identity in Christ Jesus is not determined by the affirmations we receive from a mutual admiration society, but is based upon God identifying us with Christ Jesus and declaring us righteous.

In an earlier chapter I shared with you the self-detachment teaching of Dr. Viktor Frankl. Calling a Christian away from himself unto Jesus is not a "coping mechanism" of *logotherapy* but is based upon our crucifixion with Christ. Paul writes, "I have been crucified with Christ. . . ." Separating from yourself is an action of faith motivated within us by the Holy Spirit based upon the objective facts of God's Word.

In the same manner, the teaching of the apostle Paul directing us to set our minds upon the Spirit and not upon the flesh is not a positive-thinking technique offered for the purpose of self-improvement. While it is certainly the will of God that we, his children, should live in peace and joy, the reason for the instruction to "set your minds on things above, not on earthly things" is because "you died, and your life is now hidden with Christ in God" (Colossians 3:2,3). The teaching is based upon the objective truth of what God has accomplished in Christ Jesus, not upon a desire to cope with difficult situations or a search for self-improvement.

Too Simple

When you consider some of the complicated concepts that have become associated with biblical theology, it seems too easy to claim that directing our thoughts unto Jesus will have an impact upon a person's life. To advise a person suffering from depression, fear, or worry "to think about Jesus," might be construed as rather simplistic. Yet, when you compare the teachings of Paul with the reasonings of modern psychology which offer the best of the human intellect, you begin to see that

Paul, inspired by the Holy Spirit, was way ahead of his time.

Modern psychology conceives of human life as moving in a specific direction, toward a specific goal. Abraham Maslow, who is considered to be the father of the doctrine of self-esteem, looked beyond this present humanistic emphasis to the next phase in which man moves into a transpersonal dimension, beyond self-interest, to cosmic consciousness via what he termed "peak experiences." This consciousness revolution has widely permeated the thinking of a good portion of popular, modern psychology and is at the root of the New Age movement. All of the goals for the human psyche to reach its full potential are attained via some method of expanding consciousness or controlling the mental process.

As Christians, we believe that all of human history is moving toward the divine purpose which is the full manifestation of Jesus Christ. Paul defined his ministry as proclaiming Jesus, "admonishing and teaching everyone with all wisdom, so that we may present everyone perfect in Christ" (Colossians 1:28). In Ephesians, Paul wrote that the purpose of God is "to bring all things in heaven and on earth together under one head, even Christ" (1:10). The church is to grow to the "whole measure of the fullness of Christ" (Ephesians 4:13).

The ultimate concern of the Christian is with the person of Jesus Christ. He is the measure of all things. In the centrality of the person of Jesus Christ is the identity and life of the individual Christian. Jesus Christ is not merely a historical person of the past; he is and remains a "life-giving Spirit." It is therefore certainly not trivial to claim that the conscious direction of our minds unto the person of Jesus Christ will make a profound difference in the quality of our lives. Since so many of the secular consciousness gimmicks seek to expand or direct the human thought process, how much more should Christians be taught to direct their conscious thoughts unto Jesus? In fact, when you consider the subject of human consciousness in light of human mortality, it becomes trivial to direct human consciousness at anything other than Jesus Christ.

Consider the following real-life examples which demonstrate the results of redirecting our thoughts unto Jesus.

Kicking Out Fear

A few years ago a ten-year-old girl, living in our immediate neighborhood, was kidnapped while walking home from school. As a result, the children in the local schools were instructed to be careful walking home, and to avoid contact with strangers. My youngest son, Danny, who was also ten years old at the time, became gripped and immobilized by fear. He could not sleep nights. He couldn't eat. He refused to go outside and play. Even though his school was only two blocks from home, we had to drive him to school every morning and pick him up immediately in front of the school door in the afternoon.

This went on for a number of days. No matter how much we tried to convince him that his fear was magnified beyond a normal response, nothing worked. We used the other children in his class as examples of being cautious without being gripped with fear, but it made no difference. Finally one evening, before he went to sleep, I taught him the principle of Romans 8:5,6. I instructed him to kick out of his mind any thoughts of fear that sought entrance and to redirect his thoughts and begin singing "Jesus loves me, this I know." We prayed that Jesus would fill his mind with good things.

A few mornings later he came downstairs, ready to go to school, and announced in his usual happy-go-lucky fashion, "You don't have to drive me this morning. Fear tried to get in, but I kicked it out and sang 'Jesus Loves Me.' It hasn't come back!"

No Room for Lust

One day I had lunch with a good friend of mine at the Holiday Inn in Grand Rapids. I enjoyed this man's company because we were both seeking to grow in our relationship with the Lord Jesus and live and walk in the Spirit. So we had much to talk about and would meet for lunch quite often.

While we were eating, we noticed lots of activity taking place around the indoor pool adjacent to the restaurant, but we did not pay any attention.

As we left the restaurant, we decided to walk down one of the long motel corridors to the back parking lot where we had left our cars. There was commotion in the narrow hallway, especially at the entrance to the swimming pool. Drawing closer, we found ourselves passing between two lines of beautiful, bikini-clad models. The commotion at the pool had been a fashion show. As we gingerly "walked the line" between the two rows of exposed flesh, I heard my friend mumbling under his breath: "Thank you, Lord Jesus. You certainly are a wonderful creator. You do all things well...." I couldn't help but laugh.

As we got out to the parking lot, I questioned him, "We're walking between all these beautiful models and you're declaring the goodness of God?"

With a big grin he replied, "It sure beats lust!"

Taking Every Thought Captive

Worry, anxiety, fear, lust, and self-pity are mental attitudes. They seek to gain control of our minds. In so doing, they pollute and defile us. My son Danny was gripped by an unnatural fear. My friend and I could have easily fallen prey to lust and sexual desire. As the result of redirecting the mind unto Jesus we are enabled to separate from self and experience the peace and joy of the Lord.

If you have ever met anyone who has chosen over a long period of time to entertain one of the attitudes of the sinful nature, you see the horrible results. The person who continually worries turns into a worry-wart. The person who is gripped by inordinate fears is paralyzed, unable to enjoy the blessings of life. I knew a woman who chose to hold a grudge against a relative for over 30 years. Her life, her conversation, and her demeanor reflected deep bitterness. She turned into a bitter person and defiled the lives of others by her attitudes and expressions. The writer to the Hebrews declares, "See to it that...no bitter root grows up to cause trouble and defile many" (12:15).

All of these negative attitudes and crippling emotions begin as simple thoughts seeking entrance into the sanctuary of our minds. For this reason, the apostle Paul speaks of bringing every thought captive to the obedience of Christ, renewing our minds, and setting our affections and thoughts upon Jesus. By inviting attitudes of the flesh into our minds and entertaining them, we allow them a foothold, and eventually they have their way with us. It is important to recognize that while a thought may enter into our minds without prior permission, it is our choice whether or not that thought will become the focus of our conscious attention. We can choose to redirect our thinking and turn in faith, praise, and worship to the Lord Jesus. The battleground is the mind!

11

Confessing Truth

*"The Christian faith
is not founded on beautiful thoughts
but on decisive historical events...."*
—William Kilpatrick

One Sunday afternoon I was watching a religious program on public access television sponsored by the The Church Universal and Triumphant starring Elizabeth Clair Prophet. During part of the program, Prophet stood in front of the altar in her long, flowing yellow robe, surrounded by flowers and statues and religious pictures. With fingers placed alongside her forehead, she intoned a long list of positive affirmations defining what a wonderful, filled-with-light, glorious creature she happened to be.

"I am Christ! I am Christ! I am Christ! I am Christ!" she confessed over and over again in her monotone voice. Her eyes were closed in a mystical trance, and her face was pointed upward.

My 14-year-old son happened to enter the room. He looked at the television screen for a few moments, looked back at me with a highly inquisitive expression, looked back at the close-up of Prophet's mystical countenance, and finally said, "Boy, is she weird."

I couldn't help but chuckle over the contrasting assessments of the situation. While Prophet was declaring what a wonderful, glorious creature she happened to be, declaring, "I am Christ! I am Christ!", my 14-year-old son evaluated her as "weird." I wonder whose viewpoint will be confirmed by history?

I guess the moral of the story is, if you are going to confess a high estimate of yourself, don't do it publicly. Perhaps no one will agree with you.

Positive Confession

One of the important ingredients in the positive-thinking movement is this same practice of speaking positive confessions and affirmations. The idea is to speak a positive affirmation over and over again until it becomes real in experience. Positive-thinking people offer the hope that self-improvement can be discovered by continually affirming, "Every day in every way I am getting better and better."

Clinical psychologist Dr. Albert Ellis developed in the early 1950's a therapy based upon the concept of self-talk. Ellis concluded that the reason why many of his patients did not get well is that they held irrational, self-defeating ideas about themselves. To change people, according to Ellis, it was necessary to change the manner in which they thought. Ellis concluded that human beings were verbal creatures who would silently, through the course of the day, talk to themselves. In his therapy he would instruct people to speak positive affirmations to themselves and to avoid speaking harmful, irrational, self-defeating words.[1]

The speaking forth of positive affirmations is also very much a part of the meditation technique offered in the New Age movement and in religious groups such as The Church Universal and Triumphant. When you read some of the content of the suggested affirmations, you cannot help but be impressed with the extent to which some people will go to lie to themselves. New Age teacher Shakti Gawain suggests using the following affirmations as a means for reprogramming your mental attitude:

> "I am a radiant being filled with light and love."
> "I am naturally enlightened."
> "My life is blossoming in total perfection."
> "I am the master of my life."
> "I am whole and complete in myself."[2]

Confession Based upon Fact

It is certainly the will of God for us to make a good, positive confession of who Jesus is and who we are in him. In a previous chapter, you confessed your new identity. The word "confess" literally means "to speak with." A Christian confession is spoken with God. We declare what God declares to be true based upon factual reality. When we confess, we are agreeing with God over his estimate of our condition.

Many within the church today confess only half-truths. Many of us Lutherans, for example, in our weekly confession are very willing to confess and acknowledge our sin and failure, but often neglect to confess the righteous identity that God has granted to us in Christ Jesus. Other charismatic-type groups, reacting against this negative confession, freely confess who they are in Christ, but fail to recognize that they are still dragging "ol' Adam" around with them. A true Christian confession is not one or the other, but both. What we confess is not determined by whether the confession is positive or negative. *It is determined by whether it is true or false!*

The Bible says that we have a double life. On the one hand, God says in his Word, "Because you are born in Adam, you are a sinner. Your human nature has been corrupted and perverted by sin. You are going to die." As we examine our own hearts, we confess, "I agree. I am a poor, miserable, wretched sinner!" But this is not the extent of our confession. God also affirms in the gospel, "Because I have included you in my Son Jesus Christ, you are a forgiven, redeemed, righteous, heavenly saint!" Standing firmly and confidently upon the truth of God's Word and focusing upon our identity in Christ Jesus in the heavenly places, we also confess, "I agree. I am forgiven and righteous in Christ. I am seated in the heavenly places! I am more than a conqueror. I can do all things through Christ Jesus. I believe your Word and promise."

Our confession is determined by where we choose to look. This is a very important truth which we have discussed before. If we look at ourselves, we see our sin. If we separate from ourselves and turn our back on ourselves and look unto Jesus, we see our righteousness and our position in the heavenly places. It all depends on our focus.

The Word of God: Our Tool and Weapon

Confessing and declaring the truth of God's Word is an important ingredient in living the Christian life and learning to walk in the Spirit. The Word of God, which declares the mighty acts of our God on our behalf and reveals to us our new, lofty identity in Christ Jesus, is both the tool and weapon of the Christian. As a tool, the Word is the means for the working of the Holy Spirit in our hearts. By speaking to ourselves the message of God's grace, love, and forgiveness in Christ, the very presence of God is stirred within us. We can walk in the Spirit and experience the love, peace, and joy which is in Christ. Martin Luther writes:

I still constantly find that when I am without the Word, Christ is gone, yes, and so are joy and the Spirit. But as soon as I look at a psalm or a passage of Scripture, it so shines and burns into my heart that I gain a different spirit and mind. Moreover, I know that everybody may daily experience this in his own life.[3]

As our weapon, the Word of God is the sword of the Spirit, a sharp two-edged sword whereby we defeat the temptations of the devil. Plagued by the temptation to become indulged in ourselves, we speak forth: "I have died with Christ. I no longer live. It is Christ who lives in me!" When our faith is weak and we question our identity in Christ, we declare: "God has raised me with Christ and seated me in the heavenly places. I am a perfectly justified saint in Christ Jesus." In the midst of worry or fear we speak forth: "If God is for me, who can be against me?" In times of weakness, we confess: "I can do all things through Christ who strengthens me." In the midst of a tragic situation we speak: "All things work together for good to those who love God and are called according to his purposes." When we are feeling sad and forlorn, we speak to ourselves: "Rejoice in the Lord always, and again I say, rejoice." When we are tempted to become engrossed in the pleasures and pursuits of this world, we declare, "My citizenship is in heaven!" All of our confessions are based upon the clear, full content of the Word of God.

We do not merely affirm nice, sweet, positive ideas which are totally out of line with reality. We declare to the principalities and powers; to Satan and his host of demons; to the desires of our old sinful nature; to worry, fear, bitterness, and resentment: *Thus saith the Lord!*

The memorization of key Bible passages which declare the results of what God has accomplished in Christ is vitally important to our living and walking in the

Spirit. To speak the Word in the midst of temptation, to meditate upon the Word and promises of God when passing through difficult circumstances, stirs within us the peace of God and keeps our hearts and our minds in Christ Jesus. Martin Luther wrote: "Hear God's Word often; do not go to bed, do not get up, without having spoken a beautiful passage—two, three, or four of them—to your heart."[4]

The truth of God's Word can be put before us in many forms. I know Christians who stick little "motto cards" to their refrigerator doors. Each little card expresses a specific biblical truth. Each time they open the refrigerator, they are confronted with the Word of God. I was talking to a woman recently who told me that her church in Texas gave out stickers which read: "You are looking at the problem." The members of the congregation were encouraged to place one of the stickers on each mirror in their homes as a constant reminder of the real source of their problems. In the midst of a world in which we receive so many negative messages which are not based upon truth, it is so important that our minds are programmed with the words and promises of God.

Peace in the Midst of Tragedy

One day I received the tragic news that a man in our congregation had died suddenly of a heart attack. Even though his wife, Mary, was a committed Christian, I knew it was going to be a very difficult situation. Mary was alone, since they had no children. I was also aware of the fact that Mary possessed an uncanny fear of funeral homes. She had attended one funeral in her life, from which she was carried out screaming and crying.

I arrived at their home and found Mary in an emotionally distraught condition. A number of members of our congregation were already at the home, attempting to apply some comfort, assurance, and hope. We prayed together and shared the Word together, but the combination of grief, fear, and uncertainty produced a tremendous obstacle to the application of divine promises. The issue was not one of heaven or hell—both Mary and her husband believed in Jesus, and she knew that there would be a reunion in heaven. The problem was getting through the present situation. I knew that the next day, with the initial visit to the funeral home and the open casket, would be highly traumatic.

I returned to Mary's home the next morning and discovered a totally different situation. While she was still filled with grief and sorrow over the loss of her husband, her eyes were seemingly aglow with peace and joy. Something had happened! After giving her a big hug, I looked at her eye-to-eye and asked, "What happened to you?"

"Last night," she began to explain, "I was crying out to God. 'Why Lord? Why me? What am I going to do? How will I ever make it through the days ahead?' In the midst of my crying out, I began to remember certain verses of Scripture. The Bible said that all things worked for good to those who loved God and were called by him. I remembered the verse that if God was for me, who could be against me. Rather than crying out, I began to speak these verses and to thank God for his many promises. I confessed that this whole situation would work out for good because God said it would. As I directed my mind unto the many promises of God, his peace filled my life."

I will never forget seeing Mary standing next to the open casket that night at the funeral home. Her husband was well-known in the community, so the funeral home was very crowded. While her eyes were filled with tears and they were rolling freely down her cheeks, a genuine glow of peace and joy emanated from her. Mary never repressed nor denied her grief. Yet, in the midst of her grief, by filling her mind with what God had promised in Christ Jesus, she experienced the peace which passes all human understanding. By abiding in Christ and walking in the Spirit, the fruit of the Spirit was produced in her.

Of course, such is the purpose of preaching the gospel at a funeral service. We desire to direct the minds of those who are experiencing grief to the word of the gospel which offers hope and comfort. The Holy Spirit works through that gospel, to stir faith in the midst of despair, and bring peace into turmoil.

Truth and Error

There is no comparison between the positive-thinking mentality and the biblical directions for walking in the Spirit. It is similar to comparing truth and error, substance and froth, wishful thinking with factual reality, shallow human reason with the depth of divine wisdom. We do not pull ourselves up by our bootstraps by declaring how good, wonderful, and talented we are.

Instead, when we look at ourselves we declare, "I am the problem. I am a sinner. Nothing good dwells within my sinful nature." But we don't stop there—we look up to the throne where Jesus is seated at the right hand of God and confess, "My God has redeemed me in Christ Jesus. He has granted to me the very righteousness of Christ and has already lifted me up and seated me in the heavenly places in Christ Jesus. My God is able to do far more abundantly than all that I ask or think."

12

Rejoice in the Lord!

*"You have as much laughter
as you have faith!"*
—Martin Luther

We do not speak forth the Word and promises of God in order that they might be brought into reality. We declare God's Word, because it *is* reality. We do not affirm over and over again, "I'm a new creature." "I'm a new creature," "I'm a new creature..." in order that we might be identified as new creatures. Our declaration is based on the fact that we have been raised with Christ and seated in the heavenly places. Whether I declare the truth or deny the truth does not change the truth.

When Mary declared the truth of Romans 8:28, confessing that everything would work out for good in her tragic experience, she was not producing by her confession what God had promised. Her confession did not cause everything to work out for good. Even if she would not have confessed what God declared to be true, because she was a believer in Jesus Christ and a child of God, her circumstances still would have worked out for good. But ... her experience of peace and joy in the midst of the circumstances would have been absent. I am sure you have heard a Christian confess, "When I see how well God worked everything out, I was foolish to be so worried and distraught." As the hymn writer put it, "Oh what peace we often forfeit...."

Since God has already accomplished for us all things in Christ Jesus, the attitude of faith must therefore be an attitude of praise and worship in the midst of all situations of life.

The Bible tells us: "Give thanks in all circumstances, for this is God's will for you in Christ Jesus" (1 Thessalonians 5:18). We give thanks in all circumstances because God has declared that all circumstance work out for good to those who love him and are called according to his purposes. Our joy in all situations of life is directly in proportion to our faith in the Word and promises of God. Luther said, "You have as much laughter as you have faith." And again, "We can mark our lack of faith by our joy; for our joy must necessarily be as great as our faith."[1] In Ephesians, the apostle Paul clearly defines the joyful stance of the Christian. He writes:

> Do not get drunk on wine, which leads to debauchery. Instead be filled with the Spirit. Speak to one another with psalms, hymns and spiritual songs. Sing and make music in your heart to the Lord, always giving thanks to God the Father for everything, in the name of our Lord Jesus Christ (5:18-20).

Sing unto the Lord

From the Word of God, it is very clear that singing songs and choruses of praise and worship is a vital ingredient in walking in the Spirit and abiding in Christ. Martin Luther thought very highly of music and singing in the life of the Christian and placed it right behind theology in importance. He said, "I place music next to theology and give it the highest praise." He wrote a great deal about the positive results of singing songs of praise and worship:

> When sadness comes to you and threatens to gain the upper hand, then say: Come, I must play our Lord Christ a song on the organ for Scripture teaches me that he loves to hear joyful song and stringed instruments. And strike the keys with a will, and sing out until the thoughts disappear.... If the devil returns and suggests cares or sad thoughts, then defend yourselves with a will and say: Get out, devil, I must now sing and play to my Lord Christ.[2]

When the desires of our sinful human nature cry out for attention and when the devil stands ready to bring us into worry, fear, depression, self-pity, and the like, there is no better means for turning away from ourselves and abiding in Christ than by singing a song of praise and worship unto Jesus. Anger, fear, bitterness, lust, and envy must give way to the joyful sounds of praise and worship.

I believe that some of the most positive additions to the worship life of the church have been the little choruses of praise that have become familiar to many of our people. Years ago when the little choruses of praise such as "God Is So Good," "Let's Just Praise the Lord," "Praise the Name of Jesus," and "Oh, How I Love Jesus," entered the church, some members of the clergy disdained them as being beneath their liturgical sensitivity. While it may certainly be true that these little "ditties of praise" are lacking in rich, historical, liturgical tradition, they do provide the people of God with a simple means of directing their consciousness unto Jesus. For most people, it is far easier to sing "God is so good" in the midst of times of turmoil than to intone the words of a Bach chorale.

Praise in the Midst of Adversity

If it wasn't for the adverse situations of life, the attitudes of other people, the plans that go awry, and the circumstances which are beyond our control, then turning away from ourselves and living and walking in Christ Jesus would not be difficult. Anyone can rejoice in a joyful situation. Anyone can be happy when everything is going according to plan. Anyone can love lovable people. Anyone can be at peace in the midst of serenity. But ... living and walking in the Spirit by abiding in Christ Jesus is most productive of good fruit in the midst of adversity. The fruit of the Spirit is not a gift. It is worked in us as we abide in Christ when everything is seemingly going wrong.

In Philippians 4:11-13, the apostle Paul writes:

> I have learned to be content whatever the circumstances. I know what it is to be in need, and I know what it is to have plenty. I have learned the secret of being content in any and every situation, whether well fed or hungry, whether living in plenty or in want. I can do everything through him who gives me strength.

While Paul had learned the secret of abiding in the living Christ in the midst of adversity, we are in the process of learning it.

Some years ago I was invited to speak at a conference in Florida. Since it was summertime, we hooked up the trailer and the whole family headed south. The first morning in central Indiana, we woke up to a flat tire on the trailer. While the tire was being fixed, we had breakfast. At noon, while driving through Cincinnati, a radiator hose blew. While it was being replaced, we had lunch. In the evening, as we entered Tennessee and began pulling the trailer up a long mountain, the car overheated. Since there was no place to pull off the highway, we drove the last mile with steam pouring out of the engine. Finally, arriving at the top of the mountain, I pulled over and turned off the engine. Another hose blew. All the antifreeze we bought in Ohio was dumped in Tennessee. A state trooper stopped to help us. We patched the hose and refilled the radiator with water. In the meantime, we had supper on the mountaintop in Tennessee. Since it was dark, I left on the flasher lights on both the car and trailer while we were eating. After doing the dishes and repacking the trailer, my wife and I, our four children, and pet poodle got back into the car to drive the last 50 miles to the campground for the night. As I put the key in the ignition and turned it, nothing happened. The battery had been drained by the flasher lights.

This was the straw that broke the camel's back. The children were tired and crying. The dog was uneasy after being cooped up in the car all day. My wife was disgusted, and I was mad! But rather than becoming emotionally unglued, I announced to the family that we were going to sing. Joining hands, we sang, "Praise the name of Jesus. Praise the name of Jesus. He's my rock! He's my fortress! He's my deliverer, in him will I trust. Praise the name of Jesus." As I got out of the car, a truck pulled over. The driver asked if we needed some help. He had jumper cables. In ten minutes time, we were on our way.

Singing a chorus of praise did not change the circumstances and charge my battery, but it changed my response to the situation. My initial response was a self-centered, "poor me," angry, frustrated response. As a result of singing a song of praise unto Jesus, the conscious direction of my mind changed from frustration and anger to praise and worship so that I was able, in peace, to handle the circumstances. Even though the circumstances revealed some of the anger and impatience in my heart, I was able to stand, to rejoice, to retain the "peace that passes all understanding."

All of us find ourselves from time to time in the midst of situations and circumstances which might lead us into lust, worry, fear, anger, self-pity, discontent, and resentment. In such situations, we should not fight the temptation with a head-on assault. Rather, this is the time to disconnect and detach ourselves from ourselves by directing our thoughts unto Jesus in praise and worship. As Martin Luther said, "Come, I must play my Lord Christ a song on the organ...."

Victims of Circumstances?

As much as we would like to, we will not be able to change all the basic circumstances of life. The situations that we encounter from day to day are not within our control. What is within our control is *the manner in which we respond to our circumstances.* My radiator heated up because the core was corroded, and the water was not circulating properly. I discovered that the next day. The car continued to overheat. This condition wasn't my fault. I was a victim of my circumstances. I might have tried to lay hands upon the radiator and pray for its healing, but it was too hot!

While the situation was outside my control, my response to the situation was well within my control. I could respond according to my selfish life in Adam and fall into sin, or I could respond according to the life of Christ dwelling within me. I could respond as one who is seated in the heavenly places, far above all situations and circumstances, or I could respond as an earthbound, natural human being. I could respond in faith based upon the Word and promises of God, or I could respond as an unbeliever. My response was my responsibility! This is what Jesus is driving at in his "turn the other cheek" teaching in the Sermon on the Mount. A person may respond by striking back, but in the process forfeits his peace and joy.

Because I decided to sing a song of praise does not necessarily reflect a high degree of pious spirituality. In my opinion, singing a song of praise at that particular moment was the only sensible thing to do. The time to turn away from yourself, stir up the Spirit, and act on the basis of the Word and promises of God is in the midst of unfavorable circumstances, especially when we sense the pressures of adversity beginning to close in around us and are tempted to turn in on ourselves.

In Acts 16 we read the story of Paul and Silas who had been beaten and thrown into jail at Philippi, even though they had done nothing wrong. In fact, Paul was a Roman citizen who was not given a fair hearing. They were being punished because they delivered a girl from demonic bondage. They had every reason to complain and gripe about their situation and feel sorry for themselves. God had seemingly let them down.

Instead, the Bible tells us that they were singing hymns and psalms of praise. They knew that they were being led by the Lord and that he would work everything out according to his will and purpose. By singing hymns of praise, they retained their peace of mind, their joy, and emotional stability in the midst of a negative situation. As a bonus, God opened the prison doors.

In the late innings of the fifth game of the 1988 World Series, Los Angeles Dodger pitcher Orel Hersheiser returned to the dugout after "retiring the side" and put his head back and closed his eyes. As was usually the case, his posture was picked up by the eye of the TV camera. After the game was over and the Dodgers had won the series, commentator Bob Costas asked Hersheiser, "What were you doing? It looked like you were meditating." Hersheiser responded, "No, I was singing hymns to myself so that I might quiet my mind and not become too emotional." What a witness! What a way to live!

"Poor Me"

Every month I gave private communion to an elderly woman who was confined to a wheelchair. Her name was Martha. While she certainly had her share of physical problems, she also had many blessings. Her husband was alive and well and cared for her. She had a beautiful little home on a lovely lake. She was not alone. She had relatives and friends who visited her. In spite of her blessings, I had never met anyone who was so filled with self-pity. I actually dreaded the monthly visit. If I had any joy upon entering her home, she sure attempted to quench it.

One afternoon, driving to her home, I was praying, "Lord, how do I handle this situation? What can I tell her?" I recalled the direction of Scripture to "speak the truth in love." I determined with much fear and trembling that I would, in as gentle a manner as possible, tell her the truth.

After I had interrupted her monologue of doom and gloom, worry and fear with the sacrament and was closing up my private communion kit, she started in right where she had left off. I gently interrupted her and said, "Martha, I really do not think that my visits do you much good. I share the promises of God's Word with you, pray with you, give you communion, and nothing changes. I cannot understand how you can be so filled with self-pity when you have so many, many blessings. Martha, I really think your life would be much happier if you would thank God for his many blessings rather than always complaining."

Martha became very quiet. I could feel much tension in the air. Her husband, who had been in the same room with us, quickly got up and and went into the kitchen. I bid her good-bye and left, hoping that I had not unduly offended her.

The next Sunday morning, Martha's husband, George, came to church very early. When I saw him, he gruffly said, "Reverend, I want to talk to you."

"Uh-oh, now I'm going to get it," I thought to myself. George, though he was in his early eighties, was a very large and powerful man. I invited him into my office.

"What can I do for you, George?" I asked, as if I did not know why he was there.

"Well, Reverend," he began, "You know what you told Martha last Thursday?"

"Yeah George, I do. I am sorry...."

George abruptly interrupted my apology and asked, "Why didn't you tell her that months ago?"

The beautiful thing about the story is that Martha made every effort to change. An entire avenue of ministry opened up. I taught her to reject thoughts of self-pity and believe and confess what the Bible declares about God's love, forgiveness, and protecting care. We would sing little songs of praise together at our private communion services. She died a few years later. I believe that her last few years might have been some of her happiest when she learned how to abide in Christ Jesus.

There is a warped sense of enjoyment associated with being miserable and having other people know that you are miserable. "Ol' Adam" can become a very good and comfortable friend. I used to be a part of a clergy support group which I later identified as the 4P Club: the poor pastor's pity party. We would get together every few weeks and rehearse our personal travail and ego afflictions associated with the task of "suffering through the heat of the day" in graciously serving the Lord. The last thing we wanted to hear was somebody instructing us to get our minds off ourselves and to rejoice in the Lord. Yet, that was the very thing we needed to hear.

As a result of all my self-pity and self-defending excuses in response to the criticisms of others, I wound up one Sunday afternoon as a hysterical heap on the living room floor, pounding my fists into the carpet and screaming, "I quit! I quit!" While self-indulgence might be enjoyable, it is very destructive!

"I Have the Right!"

There are times and situations when we feel that we have the right to be filled with worry, frustration, anger, fear, bitterness, and self-pity depending upon the severity of the adversity. We may grant that the person who has been paralyzed as the result of an automobile accident has the right to be bitter and filled with self-pity. After all, it is a natural human response. But the point is, *we are not naturally human people.* Paul criticized the Corinthians for acting like mere men (1 Corinthians 3:3). We are Christians in whom the life of Christ dwells. Responding to circumstances, no matter how severe they might be, by standing on the Word of God and stirring up praise will bring peace and joy into the situation.

Dr. Viktor Frankl, who teaches the concept of self-detachment, is not able to offer a relationship with Jesus as the alternative to becoming indulged in self. He merely suggests becoming involved in "meaningful activities and human relationships" in the midst of suffering. Frankl learned and experienced the principle of self-detachment in a Nazi death camp. A more horrible situation than that probably does not exist. If a Jewish psychiatrist is able to call people away from themselves in the midst of Auschwitz by offering a paltry alternative, how much more should a believer in Jesus Christ, having a new alternative life in Christ, obey the urgings of the Holy Spirit and eagerly detach from self-indulgence, no matter what the circumstances might be, and flee to Him who is our peace, joy, and hope? Choosing to flee to Jesus is not evidence of superior spirituality and Christian maturity. For the Christian in whom the life of Christ dwells, it is the most practical alternative. It is "sanctified common sense." If the life of Christ dwells within us by the Holy Spirit, it is foolish not to depend upon it.

Some years ago I led a three-night seminar in Toledo, Ohio. I was met at the airport by a middle-aged couple. As we drove away from the airport, their first words related the story of the tragic death of their only daughter in an automobile accident two years before. They confessed, "We have never gotten over it."

The second evening of the seminar, I spoke on the subject of responding to negative situations by stirring up the Holy Spirit and abiding in Christ.

The next evening on the way back to the airport, they said, "By putting into practice what you taught, last night was the first good night's sleep we have had in two years."

13

Jesus Is the Life!

*"Through Christ Jesus the law
of the Spirit of life set me free
from the law of sin and death."*
—St. Paul

When we talk about directing our conscious minds
unto Jesus, stirring up the Spirit by praise and worship,
or allowing the Word of God to be engrafted into our
confession, we are not speaking about "positive mental
attitude" or promoting a thinking technique. Such is
silliness. We are speaking about being consciously
joined each day unto the *life* that is in Christ Jesus.
Jesus speaks of himself as being *the life*. John writes,
"In him was Life." Paul writes, "'The first man Adam
became a living being'; the last Adam [Jesus] a *life-
giving spirit*" (1 Corinthians 15:45; emphasis mine).

When we teach the subject of the Christian life, we
offer the content of the *life* of Christ dwelling within us
by the Holy Spirit. Any of the principles that I have been
sharing with you regarding setting your mind on the
things of Jesus, confessing his Word, and stirring up
praise and thanksgiving are not to be viewed as laws.

They are principles governing the *life* that we received in Christ Jesus. When a hungry child sits down at the supper table to eat, he is not being good and obeying a law. He is following the principle that if you do not eat, you will not live. It is a law of life.

Life produces spontaneously. It does not bring forth results because of effort or willpower. When Jesus walked upon this earth, his behavior, attitudes, and responses to situations were not the result of a self-conscious obedience to a set of moral rules and dictates. He simply lived, spoke, acted, and responded, and his life produced the results. You may say, "But Jesus was God. He had perfect divine life within him. He didn't worry about the law." Of course this is true, but the wonderful news is that this same life of Christ dwells within us by the Holy Spirit. Think about what it means to live by this life that is within you.

The Law of Life

All forms of life possess various attributes. For example, a robin flies south in the wintertime because such an action is an ingredient of robin-life. Obviously, the action is not motivated by a conscious decision to be a "good robin" (obeying the external code for living a responsible robin-life), but is simply a spontaneous result of life. It's a law of life. The robin is not doing the law. Instead, the law is "doing the robin." If you graft a branch into an apple tree, and the life of the apple tree fills the branch, it will bear apples. It's a law of life.

Natural human life, gained from Adam, possesses various attributes. Death, sickness, emotional and mental problems, pain, worry, fear, and frustration are built in to Adam's life. Adam's life is by nature selfish, rebellious, proud, and disobedient. In addition, self-giving love, peace in the midst of adversity, joy in the face of sorrow, are most certainly not a part of Adam-life.

Paul speaks of this reality as the "law of sin and death." Adam's life does not contain within itself the spiritual standards expressed in the divine Law any more than the life of my dog contains within itself human standards, or than a petunia bear apples. If you leave Adam-life alone and allow it to "do what comes naturally," you will have moral chaos.

The life that is in Christ Jesus also contains numerous attributes. The life in Christ is eternal. The concept of "eternal life" is not a future existence but is the quality of the life received in Christ. Paul speaks of Jesus as being our wisdom, righteousness, sanctification and redemption (1 Corinthians 1:30). Love, joy, peace, and contentment are all a part of the ingredients of Christ-life. Christ-life spontaneously fulfills the will of the Father in heaven. It contains the desire for good works. Whereas rebellion, sin, and death are built into Adam-life; obedience, righteousness, and eternal life are built into Christ-life.

In John 15, our Lord Jesus refers to himself as being the Vine and to us as the branches. If he abides in us and we abide in him, Jesus promises that we will bring forth much fruit. Therefore the Christian life is, first of all, based upon a faith in Christ Jesus, dwelling within us by the Holy Spirit, to produce the quality of life that God desires for us. Only those works that proceed from a faith that looks unto Jesus are acceptable to God. Secondly, it is produced by learning to abide in Christ and walk in the Spirit. All Christian teaching regarding the Christian life must take place at the point where the vine meets the branch. Watchman Nee describes trusting Christ to be our life as a giving up of our own strength and efforts and trusting the life of Christ in us to produce results. He says:

> We refuse to act; we depend on Him to do so, and then we enter fully and joyfully into the action He initiates. It is not passivity; it is the most active life, trusting the Lord like that; drawing life from Him, taking Him to be our

very life, letting Him live His life in us as we go
forth in His Name.[1]

The life of Christ within us is productive of good
works. How does this work out in practice?

"Jesus in Me Loves You"

A number of years ago I conducted a week-long series
of teachings in a basement prayer meeting in Grand
Rapids, Michigan. One evening as the meeting came to
a close, I went over to the punch bowl in the corner of the
basement to be alone for a few minutes.

My brief moment of privacy was invaded by an angry-
looking man stomping over to the punch bowl to have a
drink.

"Good evening, how are you doing?" I greeted him.

"Aw," he answered, "I can't stand these meetings. My
wife always drags me away from the TV in hopes that I
will become spiritual."

I began to laugh. We introduced ourselves. His name
was Steve. "Why don't you enjoy these gatherings?" I
asked. "The group seems to have a good time together."

"It's all that lovey-dovey, praise-the-Lord, hallelujah
stuff that I can't handle. I'm just not that kind of person."

As we continued the conversation, he shared with me
that he was born and raised in a home where emotions,
especially love, were never outwardly demonstrated.

"I'm really not able to love people," he admitted.
"There are people that I work with that I genuinely
can't stand. In fact, I guess there are people I hate. I'm
not ashamed to say it. It is a fact."

"Are you happy with that kind of attitude?" I asked.

"Not really, but what can I do? That's how I'm made
up." He shrugged his shoulders in simple resignation to
the way things were. "Oh, I try to be nice to other people,
but it doesn't work."

"So what you are telling me," I summarized, "is that you are by nature an unloving, hateful, angry, antisocial person."

"Well, maybe I'm not that bad," he objected. "But..."

"Wait a minute," I interrupted, "tell it the way it is. Have you not resigned yourself to maintaining an unloving attitude toward other people?"

"I guess so," he admitted. "But what can I do? That's the way I am."

"Do you think that's the way Jesus is?" I asked.

"Of course not," he responded adamantly. "Jesus loves other people!"

"Do you believe in Jesus?"

"Sure I do," he answered. "I'm a Christian."

"If you are baptized and believe in Jesus, he lives in you by his Holy Spirit. The Bible says that whoever has been baptized has 'put on Christ.' Wouldn't you say that Jesus, living in you, should be able to love other people through you? In other words, do you believe that the love of Jesus for other people can come through you?"

Steve thought for a moment and replied, "I guess so...."

"Are you willing to let him do it?" I asked.

"What must I do? Remember, I'm not interested in becoming like these lovey-dovey, praise-the-Lord people," he answered quite firmly.

I explained to him that the Holy Spirit is a gentleman and in the area of living the Christian life, he works through our will.

"The key in all this," I continued, "is to get out of the way and trust the life of Christ in you to produce results."

I shared with Steve some of the important sections of Scripture, especially Galatians 2:20. I explained to him that the next morning he should reaffirm the fact that in his baptism he put on Christ, confess his failure to love other people, and trust Jesus to produce love in him. I asked him if he had any Christian worship tapes in his car. He jokingly affirmed that his wife had many of them. I encouraged him to set his mind on the Lord Jesus, affirm the truth of God's Word, fill his heart with worship, and go to work.

The next Sunday evening as I was setting up chairs in the parish hall for our weekly prayer, share, and praise gathering, I looked down the hallway and saw Steve walking toward me. He was sporting a huge grin. He came up to me and amazingly gave me a big hug.

"What in the world happened to you?" I asked.

"You wouldn't believe what happened when I went to work that morning. I was loving people! I was looking at the people in my office through new eyes. It was amazing."

This story possesses all the ingredients we have been talking about. Steve had a good sense of self-knowledge. He knew his heart. He accused himself. He was willing to detach from himself and join himself in faith to Christ Jesus by focusing his consciousness upon Jesus. The result: Steve experienced the love of Jesus.

But the truth is, Steve's natural life did not change. His human life remained the same. Steve had discovered an alternative life in Christ Jesus.

"I Can Do All Things Through Christ"

In teaching the reality of Christian life for over 15 years, probably the most dynamic demonstration that I witnessed of the efficacy of the new life in Jesus Christ involved a young woman by the name of Sally who lived in a neighboring community. Sitting down in my office one day, she poured out a sad story of fear, frustration, and failure. From her perspective, her father had never affirmed her. While her brothers were continually built up and commended, she was always told, "You never do anything right. You will never amount to anything."

Sally became convinced of the fact that she could never do anything right. This prompted within her a tremendous fear of failure which hindered her from undertaking any tasks which involved the use of her initiative and abilities. Just the week before, her husband had planned on bringing home someone from work for supper. When it came time that day for Sally to begin to prepare supper, she froze, unable to begin the task for fear of failure. Her husband arrived home and, much to his dismay, found that supper was not prepared and that his wife had spent most of the day in bed.

A friend in a prayer group of which she was a part told her that she probably had a demon of fear or a spirit of rejection. Since our congregation was considered to be a "renewed church," she figured we were into "doing deliverance," so she made an appointment to see me.

For years Sally had been involved in psychotherapy. For six months she had been an outpatient at a local mental hospital. She was a young woman in her early thirties, quite attractive but very confused. She was a committed Christian and had a "born-again" experience which, for a time, produced some very positive changes in her life. But shortly thereafter she fell back into the old patterns of fear and failure.

After pouring out the sad story of her difficult childhood, she began to cry.

"Sometimes I feel like I can't do anything right," she sobbed. "I feel like I am completely worthless."

After a few moments of silence, I responded very slowly and softly, "Maybe you *are* completely worthless."

She was startled. She looked up with anger in her eyes and said, "No one ever told me that before! My psychiatrist always tells me that I am a valuable person, that I should develop a good self-image, that I..."

"Has it worked?" I interrupted.

"Well, no," she admitted, "but I am not ready to give up on myself. I am a valuable human being."

"What if," I suggested, "giving up on yourself was the key to a new life, the key to help? Would you be willing to reject yourself if you were able to accept Jesus Christ as your alternative, as your substitute, as your life?"

I opened my Bible and for the next hour or so shared with her the biblical understanding of living in Christ and walking in the Spirit. We began with Galatians 2:20. We discussed Paul's understanding in Romans 8 regarding the "law of the Spirit of life in Christ Jesus." We looked at the section of Scripture in which we are instructed to establish our hearts and minds in Christ Jesus.

"While you may be a failure, Sally, Jesus has never failed at anything he ever set out to do!" I explained to her. "If you learn to abide in him by establishing your heart and mind in him, he will do in you what you are not able to do."

I taught Sally how to detach from herself by rejecting any thoughts that were self-centered and to live in Christ Jesus by confessing the truth of his Word and stirring up praise and thanksgiving. We talked about the verse in Romans 8 in which the apostle tells us that the "mind set upon the flesh is death, and the mind set upon the Spirit is life and peace."

I never saw Sally again after that morning. A few years later I did receive some very good news. At a pastor's conference, the pastor of one of the churches in Sally's community asked me if I remembered her. I said that I did. He continued: "Last week she was the speaker at our large ladies' gathering. She spoke on the theme, 'I can do all things through Christ who strengthens me.' She shared with us what you had told her about the truth of the Christian life."

I was amazed. This woman who froze at the idea of preparing supper was now a public speaker.

Like Steve, Sally had not overcome her problems. She had simply discovered an alternative life and a new conscious direction for her day-to-day living.

Discovering Our Need

Discovering Jesus as our life usually comes about as the result of discovering some need or lack within ourselves. As we discussed in the previous chapter, divine strength is made perfect in the midst of human weakness (2 Corinthians 12:9). Watchman Nee describes the importance of the awareness of need:

> How can we know more of Christ in this way? Only by way of an increasing awareness of need. Some are afraid to discover deficiency in themselves, and so they never grow. Growth in grace is the only sense in which we can grow, and grace, as we have said, is God doing something for us. We all have the same Christ dwelling within, but revelation of some new need will lead us spontaneously to trust Him to live out His life in us in that particular.[2]

14

Christians Under Construction

"I am not what I ought to be, and I am not what I am going to be, but praise God, I am not what I used to be!"

I can still vividly recall an incident in my life that happened many years ago. I decided to help my parents do exactly *what* they wanted, but as a result I got in a great deal of trouble. It was Christmastime, and I was ten years old. I knew that the Christmas tree had to be put up in the living room and decorated. My parents were out shopping, and I was left alone in the house. I decided to do what they wanted done. I dragged the tree out of the garage and brought it into the house. I set it in the stand, strung the lights on it, put on the ornaments, and tossed on some icicles. In my ten-year-old eyes, it looked pretty good.

But when my father came home, he was furious. Even though I had set out to accomplish exactly what he wanted, I did not do it *how* he wanted it done. Now he was faced with the task of taking it apart and putting it up the right way.

In our relationship with our Father in heaven, it is important that we do *what* he wants in the manner in which he wants it done. The *how* of God is as important, if not more important, than the *what* of God. For example, God told Abraham that he was going to become a great nation. His wife, Sarah, who in her own eyes was too old to begin bearing this great nation, advised Abraham to begin with his servant girl Hagar. He listened to Sarah and produced Ishmael. God wanted a son! Abraham did *what* God wanted, but he did not do it *how* God wanted it done. Perhaps Abraham lifted Ishmael before the Lord and said, "God, look what I have made for you. Now we can begin this great nation of ours." But this was not God's intention. It is interesting that many of the Arab nations threatening the existence of modern-day Israel claim that their roots are in Ishmael.

The Letter and the Spirit

The Bible speaks of two ways of seeking to live a good, moral life and produce good works. We can live by striving to obey the letter of the law, or we can live by seeking to abide in Christ Jesus and walk in the Spirit. We can focus our attention upon ourselves and desire to be regarded as good, righteous people who obey the law of God, or we can focus upon Jesus and desire to have his life manifested in us. We can live by law, or we can live by "the life."

Think of it in this way: A father may release his little boy at the auto repair shop while his car is being fixed, but before doing so, he may set down a list of rules. He may warn, "Don't go outside and get lost. Don't play in the grease and dirt. Don't get in anybody's way! Don't touch anything or you might get hurt," etc. If the child obeys all the rules, he is regarded as a "good little boy."

But rather than "laying down the law," the father may give his son a single instruction: "Sit here next to me and hold my hand!" By fulfilling the single instruction, the little boy will automatically obey all the rules in addition to remaining in a close, intimate relationship with his father.

God has given to us a single instruction: Abide in Christ Jesus. It is the will of God for us to live by the new life that he has granted to us in Christ Jesus. Paul writes in Romans 7:6: "We serve in the new way of the Spirit, and not in the old way of the written code." The same thought is expressed in 2 Corinthians 3:6: "He has made us competent as ministers of a new covenant—not of the letter, but of the Spirit; for the letter kills, but the Spirit gives life." Paul wrote in Romans 8:4 that the righteous demands of the law are fulfilled in those who walk after the Spirit.

In teaching the subject of the Christian life or sanctification, we do not offer the external code of the law. It is powerless to produce positive results. Paul writes, "We know that the law is spiritual; but I am unspiritual, sold as a slave to sin" (Romans 7:14). This distinction between the letter of the law and the life in the Spirit is vitally important. The fruit of the Spirit, good works, and the manifestation of the gifts and ministries of the Spirit are all spontaneously produced within the believer as a result of *life*.

Lest I leave you with the impression that the law has no purpose in our lives, it is important to point out that because of our "double life," we still do need the law, but it has nothing whatsoever to do with producing or motivating our new life in Christ. We need the law because our old sinful nature still clings to us. If a Christian was perfectly joined to Jesus in this life and always lived and walked in him, the "spirit of life in Christ Jesus" would spontaneously obey the commandments of God and bring forth good fruit. Such obedience and fruit would be the result of life, not law.

But we are not perfectly joined to Jesus. We often become indulged in ourselves and experience the temptations of our old sinful nature. If a person, for example, falls into the temptation to lust and is being led into adultery, the commandment "Thou Shalt Not!" together with the fear of being caught and possibily disgraced stand before him. In this sense, the law is similar to a safety net placed under the high wire artists. It catches them only before they hit the ground. Of course, this has nothing to do with performing on the high wire or, in our case, with the positive living of the Christian life which is not based upon the law, but upon our daily relationship with the person of Jesus Christ. The law has nothing to say to our new life in Christ which produces results spontaneously. It simply "curbs" and restricts the manifestations of our old sinful nature.

In addition, the law serves as a guide or rule which instructs us as to *what* the Holy Spirit will lead us into. Paul wrote: "The righteousness of the law is fulfilled in them who walk according to the Spirit." In other words, the Holy Spirit will not lead us contrary to the moral law of God. There have been situations, for example, in which a person has claimed that the Holy Spirit led him to leave his wife and marry another woman. This is foolishness. The Holy Spirit will not lead us contrary to the written law of God. So we still need the law, but it is not the means whereby we live the Christian life.

Disciplining Adam

It is possible to give Adam-life an appearance of being Christian by training it via rewards and punishments to submit to the law. Such training is always a chore, and does not change the content of Adam-life. It is not natural. It is similar to training a dog to walk on two legs. It can be done, but it is not natural nor does it in any way change the nature of the dog's life. Human intentions, pride, resolutions, determination, willpower, and the desire to impress others may succeed in superficially disciplining "ol' Adam" so that he behaves himself, but all you end up with is a disciplined sinner. Such positive behavior merely manifests human strength and is the source of our pride. God's purpose is to manifest Christ in us as the source of his glory! Seeking to live by the law is merely doing the right thing the wrong way.

It is very easy for us to look at ourselves and become discontented with our spiritual growth and progress and to be brought back under the guilt and condemnation of the law. Sometimes it seems as if the same old problems hang on year after year. Very often this discontent results in new resolutions and greater determination to live the Christian life, to obey God, and to do his will. Such resolutions invariably end in defeat and result in guilt.

I worked in a parish with a young lady who was always tripped up by her great desire to live the Christian life and be obedient to God. While her desire was excellent, her patience with herself left much to be desired. While God had planted an oak tree, she wanted to be a radish.

One summer she attended a seminar dealing with basic youth conflicts. She returned to the parish with her overstuffed "manual of discipline" and announced that she had discovered the way to obey God and do his will. As a result of her new resolve which produced a great struggle, her joy and peace soon disappeared. This went on for a few months until which time I asked her, "Are you ready to put away your manual and focus your attention upon Jesus?" She was. So the manual was put away, the focus of her life was directed at Jesus, and the joy and peace returned.

Letting Go

I do not think that you would deny that living the type of life I have been sharing with you would increase your level of joy, peace, and contentment. It is a desirable way to live. Seeking to establish your heart and mind in Christ Jesus by confessing the truth of his Word and promises, and stirring up the Spirit by singing hymns and choruses of praise must of necessity influence the quality of your life.

This style of life is clearly taught in the Word of God. It is God's will for us in Christ Jesus that we give thanks in all situations and rejoice in the Lord always (1 Thessalonians 5:18; Philippians 4:4). The Holy Spirit battles against the desires of our sinful flesh (Galatians 5:17). Jesus instructs us to abide in him (John 15:1-4). By walking in the Spirit we fulfill the righteousness of the law (Romans 8:4). If we learned to live and walk each day in the new life that is ours in Christ Jesus, the church would experience a great renewal. Why doesn't it happen?

Depending upon Jesus as our life means that we are no longer depending upon ourselves, and this is not easy. It is very difficult to give up on ourselves and to arrive at the conclusion that Jesus is the only source of our peace and joy. We always want to hang on to our own lives and maintain the hope that somewhere, somehow, just around the next corner, we will discover the key to happiness, contentment, and peace of mind in ourselves. But nothing ever changes. We become trapped in a way of life. It is in giving up on ourselves and turning to Jesus that we discover his life in us.

I was reading somewhere about the technique used to catch monkeys in the jungle. You drill a hole in a coconut, put some food in it, and chain the coconut to a tree. The hole must be large enough for the monkey to slip his hand in and small enough so that he cannot get it out once he grabs the food. Grasping the food, the monkey is stuck. He doesn't want to let go of the food, and as a result is in bondage to the coconut. The hunters merely collect the monkeys who by their own choice have bound themselves to the coconut.

We are often in the same position. While we long for peace, joy, contentment, and freedom, we also want to hold on to ourselves and maintain our human pride, but we cannot have both. So we are trapped! The worries, cares, and concerns of this life merely pick us up, have their way with us, and make us miserable.

Comfortable with Adam

Some of the concepts that I have been sharing with you might get you somewhat disturbed since you do not want to let go of yourself. We can become very comfortable with many of our negative responses to the situations of life. In fact, we can discover our identity in being victims of our circumstances. I knew a woman who, as a teenage girl, was given the task of cleaning up the vomit of her alcoholic father. The chore became the source of her self-pity, anger, and resentment toward life. People would respond to her by saying, "Poor Nancy, she has such a terrible life." In order to retain her "poor me" identity, she married an alcoholic and continues to clean up his vomit.

All of Adam's children enjoy self-indulgence and self-pity. If we are feeling sorry for ourselves, we can also expect some pity from other people, especially if we are willing to return the favor. One morning I was seated in a motel restaurant having breakfast and reading the paper. The booths in the restaurant had high backs on the seats so that you could not see the people in the next booth, and they could not see you. I could not help but overhear the conversation of the two women seated in the booth next to me. They were having a "pity party." First one of the women would express in vivid details all the miserable elements in her life. The other woman would interject from time to time, "Oh, honey! Oh, honey!" Then "oh, honey" would begin her monologue. As she expressed all the lurid circumstances leading to her profound anguish, the other would also interject, but she would moan, "Oh, dear! Oh, dear!" While this is a miserable way to live, it can be very enjoyable.

We also discovered as children that through our little moods, temper tantrums, and attitudes we could "pull the strings" of Mom and Dad, causing them to go along with our wishes. We never lose or outgrow this very helpful bit of information. If we are outwardly angry, we get some tender loving care because other people are afraid to cross our path. In my own situation, I know that if I am in a bad mood and growl around the house like a mad dog, I get treated much better. I also get left alone. It is a miserable way to live, but it works.

I had a woman in one of my congregations whose demeanor reflected the life-style of a "Li'l Abner" character—the little Indian who always had a black cloud with thunder and lightning over his head. A storm followed this woman into every room she entered. (It seems that every Christian congregation is blessed with at least one person of this nature.) Because she was such an angry person, everybody stayed clear of her and usually appeased her. By her outward displays of anger, she got what she wanted. Even though her self-indulged attitude placed her into a "power position" with other people, it was a high price to pay to control others. The day came when people saw through her and no longer responded according to her wishes. In fact, nobody wanted to be around her since she attempted to pull other people down with her. She found herself left alone with her own miserable attitude.

I know a man who gets what he wants because he so effectively plays the "poor me" role. If he does not get his way, his eyes droop, his voice becomes somewhat whiny, and he might say something to the effect, "That's okay. I really don't need that. I guess I will be able to get along. It will be tough, but I'll make it."

While the concept of the Christian life is very simple, the choice is very difficult. Some of you have embraced a specific way of thinking and responding to situations for the past 40, 50, or 60 years. It is certainly not easy to change your mind-set. It cannot be turned around in one day. There is a process involved. The Bible speaks of a "renewing of the mind." In Ephesians 4:22,23 the apostle Paul instructs us to put off the old man, to be renewed in the spirit of our minds, and put on the new man.

Try putting into practice some of the things we have been talking about. Guard your hearts and minds! When a temptation comes and beckons you to become indulged in yourself, do not fight it. Simply disconnect from yourself by stirring up praise and thanksgiving unto the Lord and confessing the truth of God's Word. You can find a way of escape from yourself and enter into a new life in Christ Jesus.

If you are a Christian, you have a choice. Since your will has been quickened by the Holy Spirit, you can choose to live and walk in Christ Jesus or live in Adam. You can choose to direct your conscious mind unto Jesus by stirring within you praise and thanksgiving, or you can focus your attention upon yourself. You can choose joy, peace, and contentment, or you can choose frustration, worry, and fear. The one result is found in Christ, the other is found in Adam.

Necessary Enemies

In order to shake us out of our complacent, comfortable relationship with Adam and help us make the right choice, God uses adversity. We fail to recognize that many of the little problems that are a part of our lives often remain with us *because we need them*. They remind and urge us to turn away from ourselves and turn to Jesus.

In the Old Testament Book of Judges we read that God left five enemy kings in the land to teach his people how to fight. When Israel turned away from the Lord and became proud in their own conceits, God would merely strengthen one of the enemy kings who would defeat Israel. Then Israel would repent on their knees and go forth and gain a victory. If you read the Book of Judges, you will note the same theme over and over again. While those nations left in the land were actually dead, defeated foes and were trespassing on land that rightfully belonged to the children of Israel, God left them in the land because Israel needed them. The same principle applies to us. We have our little problems and difficulties to teach us warfare and drive us to Jesus.

I knew a woman who was a committed Christian, yet her husband, Jim, was anything but spiritual. While she spent her time in church and Bible class, he occupied a bar stool. It seemed that the more she loved Jesus, the more worldly he became. She was a member of a ladies' prayer meeting and every week she would pray for poor Jim. "O Lord, please change Jim. I don't know how long I can put up with him."

As the months went by, it seemed that nothing had changed. But one day, Jim's wife discovered something. Because of Jim, she had learned how to abide in Christ; patience, peace, and love had been greatly increased in her life. She prayed, "Thank you, Lord, for Jim—exactly the way he is."

Whether it is coincidence or not, the fact is, from that time on, Jim began to change. When I left that area, he was one of the leading men in the congregation. Sometimes the very adversity that we are fighting against is the means for manifesting Christ in us.

Fruit or Frustration

Every negative circumstance, trial, or temptation that confronts us either opens the door to fruit or the door to frustration, depending upon our response to the situation. In the fifth chapter of Romans, Paul writes:

> We also rejoice in our sufferings, because we
> know that suffering produces perseverance;

perseverance, character; and character, hope
(v.3).

It seems, at least in my own experience, that the
initial response to adversity is usually on the basis of the
old sinful, human nature. I hate to admit it, but it is
true. For those of us who do not possess the maturity of
the apostle Paul, this seems to be normal experience.
While as a Christian I am in a cooperative relationship
with the Holy Spirit, my cooperation is weak and continually needs to be "kicked into motion" by the loss of joy
and peace. If, for example, I am confronted with a situation which is contrary to my plans and desires, I will
initially respond in anger and frustration. In discovering that my joy and peace of mind has been replaced
with self-pity, anger, and frustration, I arrive at a point
of contrition and repentance which will usually take the
form of, "God, forgive me for being so ignorant of your
ways and so slow to learn!" At that point, I will stir up
the Spirit so that the new man in Christ will arise again.

Twenty years ago, I knew nothing about the biblical
secret to joy, peace, and contentment, and the way of
escape. My initial response of anger, frustration, and
self-pity became a long-term response. While I blamed
others for my lack of joy and peace, I was actually the one
at fault, because I responded to my circumstances as an
unregenerate, unbelieving heathen! I was acting like a
mere man, but it was not easy to break that pattern.
Today, whenever I discover the "enemies" of self-pity,
anger, and frustration being stirred within me, I direct
my conscious mind to Jesus by confessing the Word and
promises of God or by singing a song of praise. I will not
allow harmful attitudes to have a foothold within my
mind.

Christian growth is not discovered in the absence of
conflict or in the absence of the sinful flesh. Whereas
today you may respond to adversity with long-term
anger, frustration, or self-pity, hopefully next year at

this time in the midst of the same adversity it will take you only a few moments to find the "way of escape." In some cases it may be necessary to "kick out" worry, fear, anger, and self-pity 30 or 40 times every day and turn to Jesus. But as time goes by, Christ will begin to rule over your sinful nature. The construction of the Christian life is a long-term, step-by-step process. In the same way Israel was instructed to defeat their enemies and take the Promised Land, gaining freedom from your old sinful nature is gained "little by little" (Deuteronomy 7:22). We are Christians under construction. Our motto should be, "Please be patient with me. God is not finished yet."

Perhaps the day will come when we will bring every thought into captivity to the obedience of Christ, and love, joy, peace, gentleness, submissiveness, good works, and much fruit will flow from our hearts as virtual "rivers of living water." We will be able to say with Paul, "I have learned in whatever condition I am in, in this to be content."

But for now, we are growing. We are in the process of learning from day to day to direct our conscious attention unto the Lord Jesus, to confess his Word, to stir within ourselves praise and thanksgiving. As we live and walk in Christ Jesus, good works and the fruit of the Spirit become a spontaneous production in ever-increasing measure. For now we can say, "While I am not what I ought to be, and while I am certainly not what I am going to be, I thank God that I am not what I used to be."

Interesting Results

As you live from day to day, consciously seeking to get off self and abide in your relationship with Jesus, there will be numerous interesting results. In addition to a great change in your level of joy, peace, love, and contentment, you will become very aware of of the degree to which human life in general, and your life specifically, is

directed at and motivated by self. You may be amazed by
how much of what you do, how you act, or what you say
has been prompted by how your self is being regarded
and evaluated by other people. Just about all interpersonal conflicts in which you have participated, including
husband and wife arguments, are the result of self not
being given its proper due. You will become very conscious of the self-centeredness of the people who are
around you at home, at work or in church.

You will begin to clearly discern the negative results
of turning in on self. When you feel sorry for yourself,
worry about yourself, or defend yourself, you will lose
your joy and peace. Of course, this is nothing new, but
now you will know why you are unhappy and frustrated
and know what to do about it. There are times when we
are all a little melancholy, depressed, or frustrated and
do not know why. While there may be some physiologi-
cal reasons, more often than not it is the result of
turning in on ourselves. If I find that this happens to me,
I go back and review what the focus of my life had been
over the past hours or days. I am usually able to pinpoint
the situation or circumstance which prompted my
inward turn. Turning away from self and confessing the
truth of God's Word or singing a song of praise unto the
Lord Jesus will always change the attitude of my heart.
The good news is that Jesus is always available to give
us rest.

Since you are finding your identity in the heavenly
places in Christ Jesus, you will also discover that you do
not fit the various categories that have been created by
man as a means of identifying and categorizing other
people. The only time the labels "conservative" or "lib
eral" will apply is when you are using ketchup or
mustard. Because your identity is not determined by
your theology or participation in the various movements
and anti-movements, you may no longer want to be
known as a "charismatic" or a "fundamentalist." This

does not mean that you reject or react against all external involvements or commitments to specific theological positions. Such an attitude would be self-motivated. You maintain a firm commitment to a set of doctrines which you believe to be correct and remain a part of that denomination which teaches those doctrines. In addition, you continue to love your country and honor your heritage, but this is not where you find yourself. Your identity is firmly established in Christ Jesus. A man told me some years ago, "I may not know where I belong, but I do know to whom I belong."

The New Testament directive to find our identity and life in Christ Jesus is not a simplistic solution. It is profound. The more you get off yourself and direct your consciousness unto the Lord Jesus by confessing his Word and promises and stirring up praise and thanksgiving, the more you will see just how profound it is. The person of Jesus Christ, our Lord and Savior, the King of kings and Lord of lords, our friend and one who stays closer to us than a brother, is the *only answer* to the search for personal identity.

Put into practice the things that you have learned, and you will discover that the "the peace of God, which transcends all understanding, will guard your hearts and your minds in Christ Jesus."

15

The Identity of the Christian Community

"We belong to one another
only through and in Jesus Christ."
—Dietrich Bonhoeffer

Thus far in our discussion of our identity and new life in Christ Jesus there has been an absence of any emphasis upon the role of the church and the fellowship of God's people. We have been primarily considering the relationship of the individual Christian with the person of Jesus Christ. We have not dealt with the relationship of the individual Christian with his fellow believers until now—and for good reason.

Before there can be any meaningful discussion of the nature of Christian fellowship, there must be a clear understanding of the nature of individual Christian faith and life. Obviously, the nature and function of the church is contingent upon the definition of individual Christianity. If we believe that the purpose of God is for each individual Christian to find self and develop self-esteem, the church would obviously function with that goal in mind. Alternatively, if we accept on the basis of

Scripture that it is the will of God that each individual Christian separates from self and finds his life and identity in Christ Jesus, the church would function with that goal in mind. So, we cannot talk about the will of God for the Christian community until we have clearly established the will of God for each individual who makes up that community—and this we have already done.

The Identity Crisis of the Church

The church of Jesus Christ today is facing an identity crisis. Within most denominational settings the question is being asked: "Who are we, and how do we function together?" These questions of identity have primarily been prompted by the emphasis upon the general psychological and sociological nature of group dynamics as it relates to the life of the church. Within psychotherapy, for example, the dynamic of group interaction is used as a method for developing a positive self-image and self-esteem through mutual support and affirmation. Encounter groups, "human relations," or support groups have become very popular within the church as a means for fostering closer fellowship and allowing group members the opportunity to openly share their problems and inner struggles. In addition, the very popular Church Growth Movement has made us sensitive to the sociological dynamics behind successful group operations. The problem is, these psychological and sociological dynamics have nothing whatsoever to do with a relationship with Jesus Christ. The same dynamics could be applied to the meeting of a local bridge club.

As a result of these various movements bringing to the church secular definitions of the nature of group interaction, we are faced with the prospects of losing the unique quality of the shared life of the Christian community. As is the case with the search for individual identity, the corporate identity of the church also must be established clearly in the person and work of Jesus Christ.

There is a very basic difference between the church of Jesus Christ and any other group. The nature of the life of the Christian community is not determined by sociological and psychological dynamics. The shared life within the Christian community is a result and not a cause. It is the result of individuals who have discovered their identity and life in Christ Jesus coming together with other individuals who share the same identity and life. It is not the source for the discovery of that identity and life. The source is always the individual faith relationship with the person of Jesus Christ produced through the hearing of the Word of God. In his classic little volume *Life Together*, Dietrich Bonhoeffer wrote:

> Christianity means community in Jesus Christ and through Jesus Christ. No Christian community is more or less than this. Whether it be a brief single encounter or the daily fellowship of years, Christian community is only this. We belong to one another only through and in Jesus Christ.[1]

For this reason, the fellowship of the church of Jesus Christ is not merely a mutual admiration society and does not function as a psychological support group. We do not merely "reach out and touch someone" with human feelings and emotions. Our goal is not to preserve each other's pride and build up mutual self-esteem. We relate to one another as fellow corrupted guilty sinners who have received the forgiveness of sins, life, and salvation through the person and work of Jesus Christ.

In this our final chapter, we will be considering the effect that teaching the principles of self-rejection and abiding in Christ has upon the life of the Christian church. Fellowship within the church is a vital ingredient in learning to live and walk in Christ Jesus. It is in our relationships with other people that "ol' self-centered Adam" readily sticks up his ugly head. It is not difficult to get off yourself and abide in Christ when you are away from other people. The conflicts that readily surface through interpersonal relationships demonstrate to us the damaging results of being self-centered. We learn to "get off self" and abide in Christ so that we might live in peace and harmony with our brothers and sisters.

Being involved in the life of the church is a very important subject. I do not want to leave you with the impression that it is merely an appendix to our discussion of the Christian life. It is certainly God's will for us to be a part of a Christian community in which we hear the Word of God, gather around the Lord's table, openly and honestly interact with our fellow believers, and grow together in our shared relationship with the Lord Jesus Christ.

The Church and the World

The church of Jesus Christ exists in the midst of an unbelieving world asking the questions: "Who am I? Why am I so unhappy? Where can I discover meaning and fulfillment in life?" The immediate result of teaching the principles of self-rejection and abiding in Christ Jesus is that we will have a meaningful, positive witness unto Jesus Christ.

Because we are the church of Jesus Christ, we are always witnessing. We are either demonstrating the power of God or the weakness of God; the relevance of the gospel or the irrelevance of the gospel; the life-changing reality of the person of Jesus Christ, or a set of lifeless doctrines and formulations about Jesus Christ; the love, joy, and peace of the kingdom of God, or the selfish and proud demeanor of the kingdom of this world. Being the followers of Jesus Christ, we are always manifesting either a positive or a negative witness.

When you consider the overly publicized moral failures and financial chicanery of popular televangelists, together with the incessant squabbles and divisions that take place within most Christian denominations, it is not surprising that the world is not beating down our doors in order to embrace our Jesus. In the eyes of the world, we don't look very good. As far as they are concerned, we don't have any answers. If we did, we wouldn't be in such a mess, nor would we be seeking solutions in secular psychology. By and large the people of the world look at the church and say, "Who needs it?" When you consider our witness, who can blame them?

On the local scene, most Christian congregations do not radiate the love, peace, joy, and contentment which is the fruit of a living relationship with the person of Jesus Christ. While it may be evident on the surface, if you get behind the facade, you may be surprised by what is really going on in the life of the congregation. Attending a business meeting or sitting in on the planning of a church picnic often reveals a more accurate picture of the spiritual life of a congregation than does the Sunday morning experience. Most Christians exhibit the same stubbornness, engage in the same backbiting and gossip, and manifest the same resentment, bitterness, self-pity, and frustration as that clearly evident among unbelievers. For this reason, why would anyone want to believe in our Jesus? Many pastors are often afraid of involving their new members in the politics and government of congregational or denominational life for fear that they might be turned off.

What we are experiencing in our churches today is certainly not the same style of life as that depicted in the New Testament. The first-century Christians were admired and highly regarded by the pagan society in

which they were living. Have you ever read the verses in
the Book of Acts which describe the nature of the community life among the Christians of the first century?
They are very interesting verses. It is evident that the
growth of the early church was clearly related to the
manner in which these Christians were regarded by the
world. Consider Acts 2:46,47:

> Every day they continued to meet together
> in the temple courts. They broke bread in their
> homes and ate together with glad and sincere
> hearts, praising God and <u>enjoying the favor of</u>
> <u>all the people</u>. And the Lord added to their
> number daily those who were being saved
> [emphasis mine].

Consider also Acts 5:12-14:

> And all the believers used to meet together
> in Solomon's Colonnade. No one else dared join
> them, even though <u>they were highly regarded</u>
> <u>by the people</u>. Nevertheless, more and more
> men and women believed in the Lord and were
> added to their number [emphasis mine].

In our day and age it is difficult to imagine a situation
in which Christians are admired and highly regarded by
unbelievers. I wonder how these early Christians be-
haved themselves? Undoubtedly they did not participate in the sinful pleasures of the pagan world. Yet, they
must have been a very happy, carefree, interesting
group of people who truly enjoyed each other's company
and manifested a very desirable life-style found in their
shared relationship with the person of Jesus Christ.
They had undoubtedly learned to put away self and live
and walk in the new life that had been given to them in
Christ.

It is very evident in the Book of Acts and in some of
Paul's epistles that the early church also had its share of

problems. But they were not problems without solutions. The apostle Paul always set forth the person of Jesus Christ as the source of the church's life. He wrote in Colossians 2:6,7:

> So then, just as you received Christ Jesus as Lord, continue to live in him, rooted and built up in him, strengthened in the faith as you were taught, and overflowing with thanksgiving.

The Community

The fellowship of the Christian community "in Christ Jesus" can develop into a very close and committed community of people. This closeness depends upon the willingness of individuals to reject and turn away from self and focus upon the living Lord Jesus Christ.

This closeness is very different from that experienced in a psychological encounter group. While the sense of community experienced in an encounter group is based upon the participants' willingness to take off their masks and open themselves up to one another, the closeness in the body of Christ is the result of a shared relationship with Jesus Christ. There should be no direct one-to-one relationships in the body of Christ. All relationships are "in and through" the person of Jesus Christ. The Christian community is like a bicycle wheel. Jesus is the hub, and we are the spokes. The closer we are drawn into the "hub," losing ourselves in Christ Jesus, the closer we are automatically drawn to one another.

I was a part of a fellowship of people in my congregation in New York City which was a unique group. Since it was primarily made up of the members of a Wednesday evening prayer and praise group and the Sunday morning Bible class, the same principles which I have shared with you were taught over and over again. As a result, we were all in the process of learning to "get off ourselves" and live and walk in Christ Jesus. The function of the group was directed at that goal. We defined love as helping each other to put away self-indulgence and live in Christ.

I am not remotely suggesting that we had succeeded in putting away "ol' Adam" and were experiencing a "foretaste of glory divine." This was hardly the case. Problems in interpersonal relationships continued to surface. Hurt feelings, anger, resentment, and gossip still existed. The unique difference was found in the manner in which the problems were handled. Each individual was confronted with the reality, "You are the problem, and Jesus is the solution." The task of the community was to call each other away from the misery of "ol' self-centered Adam" and direct each other to abide in the new life of Christ. As a by-product, husband and wife relationships were also deeply affected.

All teaching, counsel, encouragement, and support within the group was directed at the goal of getting off yourself and living in Christ. There was no pampering of self. Self-indulgent conversation was squelched. Those who complained about their plight in life received the usual response: "Aawwww, poor you!" On one occasion a man confessed, "I have a real problem with my pride," to which his best friend quickly responded, "We sure can't figure out why." Self was not taken seriously, because we knew that we had an alternative life in Christ Jesus. The fear of stepping on each others' toes was not the issue. Those who became a part of the group in order to impress others with their status, accomplishments, or wealth found no satisfaction.

Of course, not everyone appreciated this approach to Christian living. On some occasions people got their pride hurt, but as one person put it, "God has to continue to hurt our pride until it doesn't hurt anymore." Those who manifested a "poor me" attitude and sought pity from others at times became disturbed that they were not getting what they wanted. One man sitting in the rear of the balcony one Sunday morning actually became violent during the sermon when confronted with the truth that he was the source of his own problems and had to get his mind off himself and focus his attention upon Jesus. Yet many, including this same man, began to realize that turning away from self and embracing Jesus as your life produces a very desirable life-style. The church became characterized as a light hearted, fun-loving, spontaneous group of people who loved the Lord Jesus and truly enjoyed being around each other.

I am sure that some will ask, "What about compassion? What about empathy and being sensitive to the needs of other people?" While the Bible certainly instructs us to be compassionate and tenderhearted one toward the other, Christian compassion does not confirm a person in self-indulgence. This is detrimental to the very purposes of God to call us away from self so that we might discover our life in Christ Jesus. Genuine Christian compassion builds up the faith of another by speaking the truth of God's Word and does not simply "reach out and touch someone" with human feelings and emotions. In defining the function of the Christian community, Dietrich Bonhoeffer wrote:

> The Christian needs another Christian who speaks God's Word to him. He needs him again and again when he becomes uncertain and discouraged, for by himself he cannot help himself without belying the truth. He needs his brother as a bearer and proclaimer of the divine word of salvation. He needs his brother solely because of Jesus Christ.[2]

This past year, Judy, one of the members of the New York group, was diagnosed as having cancer. She had a kidney removed and went on chemotherapy. As a result she lost all her hair and went through absolute misery only to have the cancer reappear six months later. The support that Judy receives from her fellow members of the Christian community is very special. While she is deeply loved and many tears have been shed and prayers offered for her, she is not being pitied. Her friends are doing what fellow believers in Jesus Christ are supposed to do for each other. They are encouraging her to abide in Christ in the midst of her sickness and not permitting her to become indulged in herself through self-pity or bitterness.

Sometime ago in a phone conversation Judy said to me, "I know that if die I will go to heaven. I have known that for a long time. *But I want to thank you for teaching me how to live....*"

Fellowship Vacuum

Having accepted a call to serve a congregation in another part of the country, I truly miss the fellowship, the fun, the trust, the open and honest sharing that I experienced in my congregation in New York. As time goes by, I can clearly see the same type of fellowship existing in my present congregation as more and more people learn to turn away from self and abide in Christ.

It is a shame that those who desire open, close, honest, enjoyable relationships with other Christians are often unable to find such relationships within their local congregations. One observer of the church wrote to me recently, "In the church in which I grew up there was a tremendous emphasis on learning the fundamentals of the faith, but people were dying because they were hidden behind facades of Christianity that did not allow for honest, open sharing of very real struggles."

Traditional Christians, in their interaction with other Christians, are often motivated by the desire for self-preservation. They fear that if they let their hair down and their fellow church members begin to really know what is going on in their hearts and lives, they would no longer be thought of as "good Christians." A spontaneous, transparent Christian can be an embarrassment to other Christians who are seeking to hide their own sins and inner struggles behind a pious facade.

While we all, without exception, struggle with perverted thoughts, lust, greed, envy, and pride and also engage from time to time in questionable actions, facing and admitting our weakness is not a part of the rules for the "game of church." Even though the apostle Paul wrote that he would rather boast of his weaknesses so that the power of Christ might rest upon him, we would rather boast of self so that other people will think highly of us, considering us to be great men and women of God. I know a young man who after many inner struggles and identity problems finally discovered himself in Christ Jesus. He wrote up his story and it was published in a Christian periodical as a beautiful witness to his new life and identity in Christ Jesus. After reading the article, his family members became somewhat upset because he was willing to honestly and openly tell the world his problems. One relative responded by saying, "If our friends read this article, what would they think of us?"

In order to create openness among these "insecure" people who are diagnosed as having low self-esteem, encounter groups and support groups have become very popular additions to the programs offered in many churches. As a result, what is created is not a witness unto Jesus Christ but rather a witness unto the warm, "huggy," supportive relationships between the participants.

It is not possible to develop open, honest relationships in Christ Jesus without first teaching and embracing the principles of self-rejection and abiding in Christ. Only when Christians come to grips with the corrupted condition of their own lives, reject and turn away from self, and find their identity and life in the person of Christ Jesus, will they be able to relate honestly and openly with their fellow believers. They are willing to share their struggles not as means for seeking pity or understanding, but as a witness to the manner in which Jesus Christ has brought new meaning and purpose into their lives.

Of course, it is impossible to totally put away the personal emphasis upon self, the defense of self, or the desires of self. If this were the case, we would experience heaven on earth. But this is the goal that needs to be clearly expressed up front within the life of the Christian community. In presenting this goal, we need to tell people: "You are a miserable sinner! Your human nature has been corrupted. You are the source of your own problems. Your answer is found in the person of Jesus Christ. Our purpose in this congregation is to help you get off yourself, stop focusing upon yourself, and direct your conscious, day-by-day attention to the Lord Jesus Christ. He is your life!"

Relationships between Christians who have accepted these basic truths and agree upon the common goal are drastically changed. They no longer use each other to bolster and affirm their sense of self-worth. There is no reason to. When each individual arrives at the conclusion that "I am the problem, and Jesus is the solution," self is no longer taken very seriously, and Jesus Christ becomes the focus of attention. There is no longer any entertaining of the question: "I wonder what these people think of me?" The answer is already agreed upon. They think you are a poor, miserable, wretched, self-centered, corrupted sinner who has discovered a new life and identity in the person of Jesus Christ.

This is and always has been the very basic essence of Christianity. Jesus said, "The truth will make you free." Accepting the truth of self-rejection and abiding in

Christ sets us free from ourselves so that we may honestly approach our Father in heaven and openly relate to our brothers and sisters in Christ.

Post-Christian Era?

Are we living in a post-Christian era? Hardly! Our world has not yet seen what authentic Christianity is really all about. The present self-emphasis within our society may be a great blessing in disguise. After all, when corrupted, sinful, perverted humanity turns in on itself, it must eventually become very sick, tired and disgusted with itself. It is at that point that a living relationship with our Lord Jesus will look very good. Let us turn away from self and find our identity in Christ Jesus. We will then be *His* witnesses. We will no longer show forth what great, wonderful people we are. Rather, we will demonstrate what a great, wonderful Lord and Savior we have in Jesus Christ. To *Him* be the glory!

Notes

Notes

Introduction

1. William Hulme, *Counseling and Theology* (Philadelphia: Muhlenberg Press, 1956), p. 1.
2. Bruce Narramore and John D. Carter, *The Integration of Psychology and Theology* (Grand Rapids: Zondervan), p. 9.

Chapter One—A Challenging Generation

1. Allan Bloom, *The Closing of the American Mind* (New York: Simon and Schuster), pp. 84-85.
2. David F. Roberts, *Existentialism and Religious Belief*, (New York: Oxford University Press, 1959), p. 40.
3. Viktor Frankl, *The Doctor and the Soul* (New York: Vintage Books, 1986), p. 28.
4. Viktor Frankl, *The Unheard Cry For Meaning* (New York: Simon and Schuster, 1978), p. 21.
5. C.G. Jung, *Modern Man in Search of a Soul* (New York: Harcourt Brace, 1933), p. 201.

Chapter Two—An Irrelevant Gospel?

1. Robert Schuller, *Self Esteem: The New Reformation* (Waco: Word Books, 1982), p. 13.
2. Narramore and Carter, *The Integration of Psychology and Theology* (Grand Rapids: Zondervan, 1979), p. 11.
3. Dr. Gary Collins, *Can You Trust Psychology?* (Downers Grove: Inter-Varsity Press, 1988), p. 95.

Chapter Three—Knowing Yourself

1. Werner Elert defines Luther's understanding of the necessary preconditions for receiving the righteousness of Christ: "The righteousness imparted through justification presupposes, of course, the 'self-accusation' of the sinner. Accordingly, Luther counts it among the effects of Christ's suffering 'that man comes to a knowledge of himself and is terrified of himself, and

is crushed.' To have Christ as Savior is to need him" (*Structure of Lutheranism,* p. 85).
2. Tournier, pp. 159-60.
3. The perceptions of Blaise Pascal are very helpful in understanding the desire of man to avoid self-knowledge. Pascal recognized the vital importance of self-knowledge as a prelude to a deepened relationship with the Lord Jesus. David Roberts analyzes the thoughts of Pascal concerning the subject of self-knowledge by saying: "Thus as soon as we venture out along the pathway of self-knowledge, what we discover is that man is desperately trying to avoid self-knowledge. The need to escape oneself explains why many people are miserable when they are not preoccupied with work, or amusement, or vices. They are afraid to be alone lest they get a glimpse of their own emptiness.... For if we could face ourselves, with all our faults, we would then be so shaken out of complacency, triviality, indifference, and pretense that a deep longing for strength and truth would be aroused within us. Not until man is aware of his deepest need is he ready to discern and grasp what can meet his deepest need" (Roberts, *Existentialism,* p. 99).
4. Roberts, *Existentialism,* p. 39.
5. Ibid., p. 99.

Chapter Four—The Right Diagnosis

1. Watchman Nee, *The Normal Christian Life* (Fort Washington: Christian Literature Crusade, 1961), pp. 26-27.

Chapter Five—Identified with Adam

1. I agree with Martin Luther's understanding of the "I/self" relationship in man. German theologian Werner Elert (pp. 140 ff.) defined this relationship in terms of the "transcendental I" and the "psychic I" or the "empirical I." The "transcendental I" refers to the real person hidden beneath the perceptions and content of life. The real person exists, though only as an idea which transcends or is outside the sphere of knowledge. On the other hand, the "psychic I" or "empirical I" is filled with all the content of life, is able to be observed, and becomes the object for the reflection of the "transcendental I." This "empirical I" is the definition of "self."
2. Josh McDowell, *Building Your Self-Image* (Wheaton: Tyndale House, 1986), p. 20.
3. Paul Tournier, *Guilt and Grace* (New York: Harper and Row, 1959), p. 81.

4. While it is not possible, on the basis of Scripture, to conclusively state that Adam was not "self-conscious," the concept is both reasonable on the basis of the Genesis narrative and in harmony with the total direction of the gospel call: away from ourselves and unto Jesus.

Werner Elert in describing the "primal experience" of sin and guilt states that "the consciousness of man as consciousness of himself is in original opposition to God" (*The Structure of Lutheranism*, p. 18).

It is also noteworthy that German idealist philosopher Georg Hegel reversed the purposes of God for mankind. Hegel conceived of God as being the living, moving reason of the universe who becomes fully conscious in the minds of human beings. According to Hegel, the self-conscious human being is the fullest realization of the universe. Therefore, in describing the nature of the fall of man into sin, Hegel distorted the biblical understanding by conceiving of the Fall of man as a "fall upwards" into self-consciousness.

In *Cain, Come Home!* (St. Louis: Clayton Publishing House, 1976) Dr. Paul Bretscher stated: "Thus our very self-consciousness exhibits our alienation from our own selfhood" (p. 23).

Chapter Six—Turning Away from Self

1. Josh McDowell, p. 22.
2. C.S. Lewis, *Mere Christianity,* p. 190.
3. Viktor Frankl, *The Unheard Cry For Meaning* (New York: Simon and Schuster, 1978), p. 17.
4. Viktor Frankl, *The Unconscious God* (New York: Simon and Schuster, 1975), p. 79.
5. Frankl, *The Unconscious God,* pp. 109-11. Frankl also wrote that "self-transcendence and self-detachment are irreducibly human phenomena and exclusively available in the human dimension."
6. Werner Elert defines Luther's understanding of the significance of the cross by saying: "But faith . . . demands that we rely on what Christ did and suffered as if one had done and suffered it oneself. 'Christ is called my death.' Accordingly, it is precisely in the knowledge of Christ, in 'Christ crucified,' that the knowledge of one's own punishability and of one's own death, criticism of one's 'free will' and of one's own wisdom and righteousness, is made complete (*Structure of Lutheranism,* p. 85).
7. Paul Althaus, *The Ethics of Martin Luther* (Philadelphia: Fortress Press, 1972), p. 21.

8. Luther's Works, Vol. 12, pp. 188-89.
9. C.S. Lewis, p. 188.

Chapter Seven—Identified with Christ

1. *"When does God declare a sinner to be justified?"* This is a very important theological question. The Roman Catholic Church teaches that God declares a person to be righteous when in fact his life and behavior is righteous as a result of the infused graces of Christ. Such development of righteousness requires the purification of Purgatory. The Roman Church confuses justification with sanctification. Many Protestant Churches believe that God declares a sinner to be righteous when the sinner comes to faith. This position causes faith to be "productive," and "causative" of righteousness. From this perspective, it is not a big jump to also declare that faith "produces" and "causes" healing and prosperity to occur. Such is the distortion of the "faith movement."

   Those of us who embrace Lutheran theology believe and teach that God declared *the entire world of sinners* to be righteous in the death and resurrection of our Lord Jesus. If we are designated sinners when Adam sinned, must it not follow that we are designated righteous in the redeeming work of Christ? This is the argument of the apostle Paul in Romans 5. This teaching is called "objective justification." It correctly defines faith as being receptive of the divine proclamation rather than causing it to happen. In addition, the Christian is given a singular focus. We keep our eyes on Jesus. We do not look at our faith. We trust Jesus, not our faith.

Chapter Eight—Everything in Christ

1. Martin Luther demanded in the very strictest terms that faith in no case ever looks into itself, but only to the Christ outside of us. Concerning this demand, Werner Elert states: "Without this basic demand, every doctrine of the indwelling, no matter how it may look otherwise, would necessarily not only endanger but would actually destroy justification. The necessity for self-accusation, without which there is no justification, holds true of the whole natural and moral 'inwardness' including what the mystics call the 'depth of the psyche'.... Faith, however, clings constantly only to the other Person—the Person who I am not—to Christ" (Elert, *Structure of Lutheranism*, pp. 167-68).
2. Elert, *Structure of Lutheranism,* p. 449.

3. To gain a general understanding of the attempt to relate the concept of the unconscious mind to human spirituality, I would recommend:

> William James, *The Varieties of Religious Experience* (Penguin Books, 1982).
> Ann and Barry Ulanov, *Religion and the Unconscious* (Philadelphia: The Westminster Press, 1975).
> C. G. Jung, *Memories, Dreams, Reflections* (New York: Vintage Books, 1965).
> John J. Heaney, *Psyche and Spirit* (New York: Paulist Press, 1984).

In *Psyche and Spirit,* Heaney describes the use of the drug LSD as producing a release of "unconscious content" and thereby produces an encounter with God. This undergirds the claim of Dr. Timothy Leary that LSD was sacramental.
4. Nee, *The Normal Christian Life,* p. 127.

In describing the sufficiency of the person of Jesus Christ, Martin Luther wrote: "For in the person of Christ, there is everything, and without the Son, everything is lost. Therefore it is no small matter that without the Son, we should seek nothing and will find nothing either in heaven nor on earth, for then all is lost" (Elert, *The Structure of Lutheranism,* p. 66).
5. Luther described this reality in his 1535 commentary on Galatians: "Because He lives in me, whatever grace, righteousness, life, peace and salvation there is in me is all Christ's: nevertheless, it is mine as well by the cementing and attachment that are through faith, by which we become as one body in the Spirit (Elert, *Structure of Lutheranism,* pp. 167-68).

Chapter Nine—The Conflict

1. Luther, *1535 Commentary on Galatians,* p. 170.

Chapter Ten—Looking unto Jesus

1. Ewald Plass, *What Luther Says* (St. Louis: Concordia Publishing House, 1959), Vol. 3, p. 1345.
2. Plass, *What Luther Says,* Vol. 3, p. 1344.
3. Gary R. Collins, *Your Magnificent Mind* (Grand Rapids: Baker Book House, 1988), p. 36.
4. Collins, *Your Magnificent Mind,* p. 19.
5. Paul C. Vitz, *Psychology as Religion* (Grand Rapids: William B. Eerdmans, 1977), p. 72.
6. William Kirk Kilpatrick, *Psychological Seduction* (New York: Thomas Nelson Publishers, 1983), p. 51.

Chapter Eleven—Confessing Truth

1. Collins, *Your Magnificent Mind,* p. 19.
2. Shakti Gawain, *Creative Visualization* (New York: Bantam New Age Books, 1979), pp. 22-26.
3. Plass, *What Luther Says,* Vol. 2, p. 691.
4. Plass, *What Luther Says,* Vol. 3, p. 1485.

Chapter Twelve—Rejoice in the Lord!

1. Plass, *What Luther Says,* Vol. 2, p. 692.
2. Plass, *What Luther Says,* Vol. 2, p. 983.

Chapter Thirteen—Jesus Is the Life!

1. Nee, *The Normal Christian Life,* p. 128.
2. Nee, *The Normal Christian Life,* p. 127-28.

Chapter Fifteen—The Identity of the Christian Community

1. Dietrich Bonhoeffer, *Life Together* (New York: Harper and Row, 1976), p. 21.
2. Bonhoeffer, *Life Together,* p. 23.